Taking Sides

Taking Sides

a memoir about love, war,
and changing the world

SHERINE TADROS

SCRIBE
Melbourne • London

Scribe Publications
2 John St, Clerkenwell, London, WC1N 2ES, United Kingdom
18–20 Edward St, Brunswick, Victoria 3056, Australia
3754 Pleasant Ave, Suite 100, Minneapolis, Minnesota 55409, USA

Published by Scribe 2023
Copyright © Sherine Tadros 2023

Every effort has been made to acknowledge and contact the copyright
holders for permission to reproduce material contained in this book.
Any copright holders who have been inadvertently omitted from the
acknowledgments and credits should contact the publisher so that
omissions may be rectified in subsequent editions.

Typeset in Portrait Text 12 pt/18 pt by the publishers.

Printed and bound in the UK by CPI Group (UK) Ltd, Croydon CR0 4YY

Scribe Publications is committed to the sustainable use of natural resources
and the use of paper products made responsibly from those resources.

978 1 914484 25 4 (UK edition)
978 1 957363 47 9 (US edition)
978 1 922585 31 8 (Australian edition)
978 1 922586 93 3 (ebook)

Catalogue records for this book are available from the
National Library of Australia and the British Library.

scribepublications.co.uk
scribepublications.com
scribepublications.com.au

For my parents, who told me a long time ago that if I was going to put them through hell, I should at least write a book about it.

'As for the activists, we always find a way.'

~ Alaa Abd el-Fattah, British Egyptian activist, writer, father, friend. Unjustly imprisoned in Egypt.

Contents

Author's Note

These are stories from my life, told the way I remember them. I tried my best to stay true to the details and emotions, even when they were difficult to recount. Some names have been changed to preserve anonymity, or just because I'm bad with names. Some details or people have been omitted, and dialogue approximated, to keep the pace, but never at a cost to the truth.

The aim throughout is to inspire you to think about how to change the world, and make you believe that you can.

PROLOGUE:

The Interview

The bright bathroom lights weren't helping my confidence as I stared at myself in the mirror. I still looked tired, despite the layers of foundation I'd applied to fill in the dark semicircles under my eyes. My mother had tried her best that morning to straighten my thick, curly hair, but the bits around my face had already started to frizz. I tried to focus on counting my breaths. Four seconds in, hold, exhale for longer, just like I was taught. I didn't have much time, and I needed to get it together. I was at the London headquarters of the largest human rights organisation in the world, and I had one shot at convincing them to hire me.

But this was not where I had thought I would be today. I was meant to be at home in Cairo, waking up next to him, still giggling about the night before and recounting stories of the funny things that had happened. I was meant to be wearing my new white 'Mrs' pyjama shirt and getting excited about having brunch with family who had flown in to be with us for our special day.

Instead, here I was. Alone, with grief overwhelming my entire body, in this overlit bathroom. I moved my right thumb to the back of my ring finger. For the past year, it had been what I'd done in difficult moments to calm myself. I'd twist the thin bit of metal until I sensed the sharp edges of the diamond and then push it back around again. It reminded me that somebody loved me, that a new life was awaiting me.

Now, rough skin had replaced the feeling of my ring, another cruel reminder of what I had so suddenly lost.

I heard a knock on the door.

'Are you ready for your interview, Sherine?' said a voice, with a mixture of confusion and concern. 'They are all waiting.'

I had asked to use the bathroom as soon as I arrived in the building, fifteen minutes ago. I wasn't sure it was a good idea to sit in a waiting room; I wanted to avoid people for as long as possible.

'Yes. I'm ready,' I answered, grabbing the handle of the bathroom door and letting myself out. I was led up two wide flights of stairs and into a conference room.

'Sherine Tadros is here to interview for the Head of Office position at the United Nations,' announced the woman as she opened the door, revealing a large man wearing a brightly coloured African shirt known as a dashiki, and a slight woman with fine brown hair. They were both sitting behind a long desk. On the wall behind them was a photo of a life raft in turbulent waters, filled with terrified women and children holding on to their belongings. In the corner of the photo, '#IStandWithRefugees' was written in big black letters against a yellow background. I recognised the hashtag as one of the organisation's main campaigns.

I sat down in front of the two interviewers and realised there was a laptop on the desk with another man's face staring right at me. He had a wide smile.

'Our colleague from the Kenya office is joining us on Skype for the interview,' the woman with the fine hair explained.

She introduced herself as Audrey, head of the refugee and migrants team. I recognised the man next to her with the African shirt: I'd spoken with him on the phone a few weeks earlier when I was thinking of applying for the job, and he had patiently talked me through the steps. He was much taller than I had imagined, with a round, full face that was imposing yet gentle. His name was Tawanda, a prominent Zimbabwean lawyer and human rights advocate who was now a senior director.

'I'm glad you reached out and could make this interview. What a lucky coincidence that you are in London today!' Tawanda said.

Lucky, I thought. If he only knew the truth of why I was here, how my life had been ripped away from me without warning two days ago. How I had spent most of the time since in bed, on a cocktail of anxiety medication and sleeping pills, numb to the world.

'Thanks. Yes, very lucky,' I answered, trying not to make eye contact.

For the next hour, the three interviewers took turns asking me questions. My body started to relax, my hands let go of the arms of the chair, and my back sank into the hard plastic supporting it. This was familiar territory, being asked questions and having to think quickly while looking thoughtful. For the past decade, I had been a foreign news correspondent, covering wars and conflicts across the Middle East for two big television networks. I had learned to keep my cool in front of the camera, crafting clever answers to complex questions even when I could barely hear them over the sound of gunfire or the shouts of pro-testors. I knew how to shut everything else out: conflict reporting is about looking in control when you are anything but, and I had mastered that art.

As the interview went on, I became more animated. For the first time in days, I felt like myself. I was almost enjoying it. My mind was busy picking the right words and arranging them in the perfect order. I didn't have to work out what to do about the mess my life was in; I just had to focus on what to say next.

Audrey was asking me about the growing Syrian crisis that had arrived on Europe's shores. It was mid-2016, and according to the UN there were now over four million Syrian refugees. The world had been shocked into action the previous year after seeing a photo of the body of a two-year-old boy called Alan Kurdi, who had washed up on a Turkish beach as he and his family tried to reach Greece. I had been there. Deployed to the beach that afternoon to report the story, I had found one of the guys who were first on the scene and who had taken photos of Alan's dead body. The toddler's blue shorts were by his ankles and his nappy was barely hanging on, covered in kelp. He was face down in the sand, but you could still see red marks on his cheek. I remember thinking about the more sanitised photo of Alan that went viral. Perhaps that was the only way to make people care about what was happening — to clean him up and hide his brown, scarred face so that Western mothers and fathers could imagine him as one of their own, rather than just another desperate, dark-skinned child.

One of the interviewers asked me what the refugees I had spoken to wanted from the international community, and specifically what the UN could do to try to help them. These were the kinds of questions I had been asking myself for a long time, and the answers came easily. They were more relevant and important than the sterile questions I had spent years being asked by news presenters sitting in studios. I answered honestly and simply: The refugees wanted to go home safely. In the meantime, they wanted to be treated with dignity, and for their basic rights to be respected in their host countries.

The final question was one I had prepared for, but somehow it still took me by surprise.

'Why do you want to leave journalism for activism? You're the Middle East correspondent for Sky News. That sounds like a job many people would want,' Tawanda said.

Fair question. I was at the top of my game, my team had just won multiple awards, and there was no way this new job would offer anywhere near the salary I was on.

Part of the reason I wanted out was that I was exhausted by the constant travel, by living in dangerous places, by the daily stress and pressure. And I was afraid of the person I was turning into. But that wasn't the whole truth.

'My job ends at the wrong point,' I replied, realising as the words came out that I wasn't making sense, a suspicion confirmed by the look on Tawanda's face.

'What I mean is,' I went on, 'I ask questions and try to expose what's going on. It's a necessary and important job. But then I leave and move on to the next story before anything is done. Before the refugees resettle or go back to their homes. I'm tired of reporting and moving on. I want it to be my job to do something about the suffering I've witnessed.'

I had spent over a decade working in the media and come to a simple realisation. There are many worthy and valid reasons to want to become a journalist, but those were not the reasons why I decided to become one. Once I'd realised that, there was no turning back. There was something else I was meant to be doing.

In the process of making change, we all have different roles to play, different callings. Perhaps because I now felt I had lost everything, I had finally found the courage to pursue mine. I didn't just want to expose injustice, but to fight it.

I hoped that my answers had impressed the interviewers, and that my passion made up for the obvious gaps in my knowledge. I was asking them to trust me to lead their team of advocates at the United Nations in New York, and represent the organisation at meetings and during negotiations. The truth was I had never set foot inside the UN building before and knew very little about what the UN even did. I had not fully understood many of the questions they had asked me. I had no knowledge of international law and the rules of war, nor had I even read the Universal Declaration of Human Rights, the principles the organisation was founded on. But the years I had spent in war zones had given me another kind of knowledge: I knew about the pain of a mother who had lost her son in an illegal airstrike, and the unfairness of fleeing your home and seeking refuge in another country, only to be treated like a terrorist. I wanted to help put right the injustices, and ultimately to see someone held accountable for the crimes I had witnessed, crimes the world was in danger of forgetting.

We finished the interview, and I went back down the stairs

towards the building's exit. When I got to the bottom, I noticed a long wall that had been turned into a blackboard. I had completely missed it on the way in, distracted by the task ahead of me. At the top of the board were the words, 'If you could make one wish for the future ...' and underneath staff had written down their answers in coloured chalk. Their visions for what a just society looked like. All the different ways they wanted to change the world. I suddenly felt lighter, like I wasn't an intruder here.

As I read the answers scattered all over the wall, laughing at some of the comments ('office puppies' and 'free office doughnuts' among them), I felt a hand on my shoulder. It was Tawanda.

'You were very impressive in there,' he said. 'We still have to discuss and go through the formal channels, but we would be honoured to have you join us.' He continued in a more sombre tone, 'The only problem is that we need someone in New York right away, and I know that you had said ...' He stopped suddenly, his eyes widening, as though he had just remembered a crucial bit of information. 'In fact, didn't you just get married?'

'No,' I replied, so casually that Tawanda must've assumed he had mixed me up with someone else. 'I'm actually ready to leave for New York as soon as possible.'

Tawanda looked pleased and reached out, grabbing my hand and sandwiching it between both of his.

'Well, then, welcome to Amnesty International,' he said proudly.

As soon as I walked out of the building, a car pulled up. My parents were in the front seats, and squashed in the back were my older brother and sister and my good friend Leila. They had travelled overnight to London, leaving their kids and jobs without notice, just to be with me. I approached the car and felt my eyes moisten, this time not so much because I was sad but because of the love I felt looking at all their worried faces. They were scared I wouldn't be able to handle another disappointment.

'How did it go?' my sister shouted out of the window.

I told them what Tawanda had said, and my mother immediately jumped out of the car and threw her arms around me tightly, tracing the symbol of the cross on the back of my shoulder with her thumb as she whispered, 'Thank God.' I imagined her praying silently in the car for the past hour, barely listening to anyone. My brother looked over and smiled. He said, 'Nice one, Sher,' as though I had just scored a goal at one of our childhood Saturday football games.

'It's not official yet, so we shouldn't get excited. These things can fall apart, and I haven't seen the offer yet,' I said forcefully, realising that I should probably have led with that disclaimer.

I looked over at my father, sitting in the car and watching me from the side mirror. As usual, it was hard to read his face, but I thought I saw him smile.

'God will do what's best for you,' he replied, sounding so certain it gave everyone permission to return to the celebratory mood. 'Let's go,' he said, starting the engine.

1.

Number 29

It never occurred to me that God didn't exist. Growing up, it seemed like He was the one making all the decisions. If I wanted to see my friends, my parents replied in Arabic, 'Insha'Allah,' — 'God willing.' When it was something bigger, like buying a bike, they said, 'B'izn Allah,' — 'With God's permission.' His presence was one of those things I accepted as a child without question, like being told to brush my teeth every morning or not to play with my food.

After all, God was everywhere in my house. Little plastic and wooden replicas of Jesus were all over the living room and bedrooms. Assorted statuettes of saints, often fighting lions or dragons, crowded the top of the piano, fireplace, and side tables, scattered between framed baby photos of my brother, sister, and me. They appeared in pictures on the walls, too, and were attached to the fridge with tiny cross-shaped magnets. I never saw my parents buy them, yet these little invaders kept multiplying and occupying any space they found. They watched as we ate or played, looked down at me as I climbed up the stairs. The big blue eyes of the Virgin Mary followed me from room to room. 'It's for protection,' my father told me. *From whom?* I wondered silently.

For 26 years I lived in my parents' house, barely spending a night away from them. Our home was house number 29, on the corner of a private road and a quiet street where trees and shrubs sat politely, separating neighbours who knew each other's names but not much else. The neighbourhood, St John's Wood, was walking distance from my preschool, which was run by nuns. My girls-only secondary school was a short bus ride away. University was just a few stops further, not far from our church, St Mark's. Observed by Biblical characters and swaddled by affluence, my life back then existed within the confines of a few pristine London miles.

But my childhood was also wrapped in the culture, sounds, and aromas of the Middle East. My father insisted on speaking Arabic at home, pretending not to hear me if I asked him a question in English. My mother always cooked Egyptian food, even when we had English guests over. Even when I begged her not to.

It was only when I started making friends at school that I realised how different my family was. I remember the first time Emily — the most popular girl at my primary school — came to my house. Emily had silky blonde hair. When the wind blew, the fine, straight strands fanned around her head and landed perfectly back in place, like she was a princess. Not me. My hair was black and thick; the wind did nothing to it. The only way to tame it was to slather it in greasy creams and tie it back in a bun so tight I felt as though my forehead was being stretched like a canvas. Before Emily arrived, I went around the house removing as many Egyptian artefacts as I could, hiding the Jesus replicas and icons in my school bag. I even tried to mask the sharp smell of incense by lighting scented candles I found in the bathroom. I'm not sure if my parents noticed me doing this, but if they did, they never mentioned it. Maybe they just put it down to the peculiarity of their youngest child, who cared so much about what everyone else thought.

But it wasn't just me who cared. We were living in a country that was openly hostile towards immigrants. As Margaret Thatcher famously explained the year before she was elected prime minister in a landslide victory, Britons were afraid of being 'swamped by people with a different culture'. The 1980s in the UK were marred by economic crisis and the continued rise of far-right groups, as well as widespread riots protesting against racial discrimination, specifically by the police.

One Sunday after my ninth birthday, my family and I arrived back home from church to find an elderly English woman, with hollow cheeks and thinning white hair, standing on her balcony overlooking our garden and shouting at us. She told my father to go back home, that Arabs were not welcome in the United Kingdom, and that my family had no right to be there, stealing jobs. The wrinkles on her face grew more pronounced as she spoke; her throat tightened and her voice strained with her determination to have her say, despite a nasty cough punctuating every few words. I had never seen anyone so angry.

My mother hurried me and my brother and sister inside. 'Baba is coming,' she said, shutting the door behind us. 'He's just unloading the car.'

'Don't worry, that woman is unwell,' she offered uncon-
vincingly when she saw us looking worried. Closing the subject,
she instructed us to continue singing the song we had practised at
Sunday school that morning. It was in Arabic, and I didn't understand all the words, yet after weeks of memorising they now came
easily to me. I wanted to go outside to defend my father; I wanted
to shout back at the old lady who was being mean and unfair.
Instead, I stayed inside with my mother and sang, surrounded by
the familiar smells, grateful to be inside Number 29 with all the
little plastic Jesuses and saints around me.

I knew then that I didn't wholly fit in anywhere. In London, I
was an unwelcome visitor. I often mispronounced my own name
— *Shur-reen* rather than *Shir-een* — when I was asked what it was,
just to make the person in front of me feel more comfortable. In
Cairo, where my extended family lived, my cousins teased me for
having an accent when I spoke Arabic. They called me *khawaga*
— the foreigner. I looked Egyptian, I sounded British, and, with
a blend of gentle joking and harsher mockery, my school friends
called me a *halfie*.

My parents made sure we visited Egypt as often as possible
and for as long as possible. We flew out the morning after school
break started and returned the night before the term resumed.
I never understood why my teachers got so excited when I told
them where I was spending my holidays.

'Just Egypt,' I'd inform them casually when they asked,
watching their eyes widen. 'I've been going since I was a baby,' I'd
add, to stress that it wasn't a big deal.

The visits were a welcome break from the monotony of
school, and I eagerly awaited them during the cold, dark months

in London. Summers were spent slowly baking on the beaches that lined the Mediterranean. Weddings and birthdays brought the whole family together. Egypt was where I had my first crush on a boy, where I first straightened my hair, and first drove a car.

My parents felt more in control in Egypt than in England, and were more willing to let down their guard. In Cairo, I could knock on the neighbour's door and play for hours with my friends without supervision, and I was given treats without even asking. I was allowed to buy my favourite chocolate from a stall near the house anytime I wanted. It was called a Rocket — a ridiculously hard caramel ensconced in a thick layer of milk chocolate. I must've lost at least three of my baby teeth in them.

In Egypt, love felt easier; generosity was uncomplicated. But it wasn't always fun. Egypt was also where I watched my aunt deteriorate and pass away from cancer, and where I saw my father cry for the first time, at his mother's funeral. Egypt was where I witnessed kids eating out of garbage trucks and old ladies on the street begging for food in the blistering heat, too dehydrated to cry. I sat comfortably in my air-conditioned car while they placed their hands on my window and mouthed, '*Sa'deeni*,' — 'Help me.' Egypt was where for the first time in my life I got so angry that I started shaking, watching a man beat a donkey until the gutters filled with the defeated animal's blood. It was where I first felt shame, when a woman on the street called me a prostitute for wearing shorts. I was six. Just as love and grief were raw and unvarnished in Egypt, so too was the ugliness of humanity.

At least once a year, my parents made us visit a monastery on the outskirts of Cairo. It's normal for Coptic Christian families like ours to make these types of pilgrimages. The Coptic Church is an ancient Orthodox religion that has been around since the first century. Copts account for more than 10 per cent of the Egyptian population and form the largest Christian sect in Egypt.

The monastery we visited was where Simon the Tanner, a highly venerated saint in the Coptic Church, had his shrine. To get there, we passed through an area known as Garbage City, a sprawling wasteland that, over the last five decades, has been home to thousands of mainly Coptic Christian families. They live among the mountains of trash and earn a living from sorting and recycling it. Just about every foreign journalist who lives in Egypt will eventually end up doing a story on the people who live among the garbage, called *zabaleen* in Egypt, literally meaning 'the garbage people'. Some have used their story to describe Egypt's deep poverty, others to point out its entrepreneurial spirit. Sometimes the *zabaleen* have been used as an example of how Muslim and Christian communities can live side by side.

My father would drive down the narrow paths of Garbage City, the car swaying left and right like a boat in rough waters. Layers of flattened plastic and metal cans lined the roads as young children with dirty faces and dogs with missing limbs slid by the windows.

Sometimes my mother would tell my father to stop the car, and we got out to give people clothes and other belongings we no longer needed. We braced ourselves for the smell that forced its way into the car as soon as the door opened — a steaming mix of rotten food and mould that quickly overwhelmed our cool, air-conditioned space.

I often insisted on going outside with my mother while the rest of my family stayed in the car, standing next to her as she handed out used toys and shoes to the children. She would ask them to line up, smiling back at their eager faces as she took the goods out of a large bag, like Santa. The children walked off cradling T-shirts or sandals in their arms as if they couldn't believe their luck. It was strange to watch; these things that had once belonged to me and my siblings, things we had discarded when they were no longer clean or new, were now precious treasures for these kids.

Once, at my mother's suggestion, I took some Rocket bars with me for the kids. I gave them out, watching huge smiles appear on the kids' faces as they undid the wrappers and quickly took in the sweet smell of the caramel before it got lost in the odour of the dead rats and refuse around them. As soon as the chocolate was exposed, swarms of tiny black flies surrounded their faces, but the kids didn't mind, swatting the insects away as they bit into the bars.

There were photos of Jesus everywhere in Garbage City. Held up against planks of wood with bits of sticky tape, sitting neatly in huge glass frames nailed to the makeshift walls. Jesus, with his blond hair and deep-blue eyes, looked strange amid the unkempt surroundings. Just like me, these kids had grown up surrounded by plastic saints and church songs. Yet nothing about the place felt familiar. My grandmother's jasmine-scented house in Cairo was just thirty minutes away, but even the flies there didn't seem as aggressive.

The visits to Garbage City made me feel deeply guilty — not only because the people there were poor and I wasn't, but because I walked away when I'd had enough; when the smell overwhelmed me and I craved the car's air conditioning. I couldn't articulate it then, but I knew that I wasn't doing my part to address the inequality in front of me.

This guilt returned again and again as I got older. Even though I enjoyed my holidays, there was something harsh about Egypt that made me thankful not to live there. The poverty in Garbage City; the incessant crowds; the callousness with which the police handled street beggars; the way schoolkids were packed inside busted buses with no doors, sitting on each other's laps because there wasn't enough space — it gave a disturbing impression that people in Egypt somehow mattered less than in other places. It seemed impossible for a person there to have real agency or choice over their future — especially if they were poor.

I quickly learned the privilege of having a British passport in Egypt and, perhaps even more advantageous, a British accent. There were distinct benefits of people thinking maybe I wasn't fully Egyptian — of being *khawaga*. I couldn't understand how so many Egyptians reconciled their strong nationalism with what seemed like an intrinsic assumption that all things Western were superior. Pale skin, light eyes, dropping English and French words into everyday conversation — these alone were seen as signs that you belonged to a superior class.

My parents grew up in that rarefied community. They came from the two big Coptic families occupying the long stretch of road from the main airport to downtown, and their family homes sat at opposite ends of the same street in one of the wealthiest neighbourhoods in Cairo. The previous owner of my father's house was a wealthy and notoriously corrupt politician. After my father and his family moved in, they found two hidden rooms, which had previously been used as torture chambers.

Although my father and his siblings were born in Cairo, they never forgot where their forebears came from, nor the sacrifices that afforded their education and comfortable living. My grandfather and generations before him were from Upper Egypt. They had processed and cleaned cotton, preparing it for use in the textile mills. These were hard-working men, traders who grew up on cotton fields nourished by the River Nile. It was a big deal for the family to own property in Cairo.

It was this sense of duty to his family that pushed my father to get a degree in dentistry, despite having little interest in the profession. Back then, your degree wasn't about what you would be studying so much as the title and social status it gave you. When my father became a dentist, people called him Doctor Ihab; his brother studied engineering, so they called him Engineer Doss. Those were just about the only two options for respectable middle- and upper-class men back then.

My mother grew up with her parents and four brothers in a house that looked more like a fortress; the house and its acres of land were manned by an army of gardeners, maids, cleaners, and cooks. They even had a full-time ironing man, who I never saw in real life. I remember my grandmother would only need to shout, '*Ya maquagy*,' and perfectly pressed shirts smelling of burnt starch would appear in the arms of one of the maids. I thought that was the guy's name, Maquagy. It took me years to realise it was Arabic for someone whose profession is to iron.

One aspect of life that cut across social class in Egypt was political oppression. The extent to which you experienced it differed according to your means; at the same time, there were red lines nobody could cross. The most obvious was criticising the president, Hosni Mubarak, who took office the year after I was born. His photo was the first thing I noticed on landing at Cairo airport from London. There were images of the president on the walls, watching over all who came into and left the country. His photos were abundantly scattered around public buildings in the same way the religious figurines decorated Number 29.

I don't remember how I knew that I shouldn't say anything bad about Hosni Mubarak; it was just another one of those pieces of information I inherited. Mubarak's security apparatus had networks of informants infiltrating not just official spaces, but some private ones, too. It wasn't always safe to speak freely. People who were seen to be out of line would often be invited by officials for a 'chat', where they were served warm tea and an icy warning. That was how Mubarak and his regime maintained an environment of fear and control.

Once, when we were on holiday in Cairo, gathered at my grandmother's house, the youngest of my mother's four brothers, Adam, went missing. He was in the middle of his three years of compulsory military service, which he served at an army base not far from the capital. He didn't come home at the usual time one night, and my grandmother started panicking. Adam was the fiery brother — not a radical, but someone who spoke his mind about politics and corruption, much to my grandmother's dismay.

She immediately called her eldest son, my uncle Ayad. Since my grandfather's passing two years earlier, Uncle Ayad had taken over the family business, an architecture company that worked on massive infrastructure projects for the Egyptian military. Over the years, Uncle Ayad had accumulated contacts within an otherwise closed circle of military officers who only trusted each other.

By the time Uncle Ayad arrived, we were all in tears. My mother and grandmother were sure something terrible had happened to Adam. I didn't understand what was going on; every time my mother started to say something about the government or the military, my grandmother shushed her. 'Not now,' she kept saying.

Uncle Ayad walked into the living room slowly, stopping to kiss me and my siblings on the forehead. He joked about how tall we were getting and the specks of black my brother was calling his moustache. Uncle Ayad was a tall man with a heavy presence, but there was a gentleness to him that was warming. He eventually made his way to the phone in the corner next to the large dining table and dialled a number, sighing deeply as the faint sound of the ring filled the room.

Moments later, he was smiling and joking with a man he called Liwwa.

'Who is Liwwa?' I asked my mother.

'It means "major general",' she answered quickly, eager not to miss any of the conversation.

After a few minutes, Uncle Ayad hung up the phone and turned to my grandmother. 'He's fine,' he announced. 'They just wanted to talk to him about something. He will be home in an hour, *insha'Allah.*'

My mother collapsed into the chair, taking the three of us in her arms and squeezing us tightly. My grandmother, meanwhile, began talking about what a great man the major general was, what a good friend to the family he had always been. After the excitement started to dissipate, we got into the car and headed back to the house where we were staying.

It was getting late. Everyone looked relieved and happy, but I was desperately confused. My anger with the regime and the military lingered. They had unfairly taken Adam away, and we didn't know why. Then, just hours later, we were thanking the major general and bestowing our best wishes on him and his family. Weren't these the same people who had taken Adam away? The same system that allowed us to believe something terrible had happened to him without reason? What about the people whose relatives disappeared but who didn't have the major general's number?

I wondered whether my mother was having these same thoughts, whether her smiles were real. I caught her reflection in the window; she was mouthing something with no sound. When I asked what she was doing, she told me she was praying because she was grateful.

'Grateful to the major general?' I asked her.

'No,' she shot back, as if angry with the idea. 'Grateful to God for returning Adam to us safely.'

I guessed that was how she reconciled herself to what had happened — by thanking God and believing it was His doing that had returned Adam, instead of the major general's. Perhaps she thought it was the only way to survive in Mubarak's Egypt. Perhaps she was right.

It was this oppressive atmosphere that had made my parents leave their comfortable homes in Egypt and emigrate before I was born. My father had moved to London when he was 21. He barely spoke English or knew anyone in the city, but he was determined to make his own way — driving taxis and performing odd jobs to make ends meet. Eventually, he was able to afford a small property in London's King's Cross, which he turned into a fish-and-chip shop called Dish & Dash.

I used to make my father repeat the story about D&D to me over and over again. About how shocked my mother was when they got married and she moved to London, only to find herself serving greasy fish to old English men on Friday nights. Once, a drunk man came into the shop, ordered a plate of chips and then proceeded to shout racist slurs at my parents, eventually throwing the chips at them. They landed smack in my mother's face.

My parents persisted with the shop, set on making enough money to move into a better apartment. Then, one day in London, a church acquaintance who had come from Sudan made my father a proposition. It was the late 1970s; the Sudanese government had started to open up the country after the defeat of the Sudanese Communist Party and the end of a 17-year-long civil war. There was a growing market for Western goods, but few people had the language skills and contacts to meet the demand. This acquaintance had secured import licences from the Sudanese government and asked my father to be his supplier. Before long, my father was doing deals with well-known brands and companies across Europe — exporting everything from toothpaste to sardines to Sudan.

With the money coming in from my father's new business, my parents bought a small apartment in North London, where my sister was born and, shortly after, my brother. By 1980, my father had become the main agent in sub-Saharan Africa for both Heinz and Heineken — supplying factories in Khartoum and Addis Ababa with canned goods and beer. With business booming, my parents were able to move up in the world, and they bought Number 29 a couple of months after I was born. My brother and sister like to joke about the fact that I only came along after the tough immigrant years were already over; unlike them, I never experienced the hustle. I was born into comfort.

———

My sister, Rania, was five years older than I was, and much smarter. She excelled at everything she tried at school, leaving an impossible-to-replicate list of accolades behind her. It felt like I was in a constant and unwinnable race. Rania was the head girl of our school and captain of the debating team. The only thing she wasn't interested in was sports, so that became my strength — the one thing I could be good at without being overshadowed by her. I was an avid runner and I loved football, especially because it was something I could share with my brother. Every Saturday that I can remember until the day I left home, my older brother, Rafeek, and I played soccer in the park with his friends. We put up two large plastic goals and stayed for hours. Even on the day of my sister's wedding, Raf and I played until an hour before the ceremony, returning home with bloodied knees and grass in my hair. I'd never seen my mother so angry.

'I didn't know I gave birth to two boys!' she shouted, as I sprinted up the stairs to shower.

Rania was the reliable one, incapable of making mistakes.

When I got upset at my father for spending so much time working abroad and leaving us in London, it was my sister who explained to me that the travel was the price we paid for our toys, the indoor swimming pool, the safety he had created for us in a country that wasn't ours.

She seemed to understand this even better than my mother did. Rania was always the one to know when my father was going on a work trip and when he was coming back — he told her information like that, delegating the delivery of the news to the rest of us. She graduated from King's College London with a law degree and got a job as a solicitor with one of the largest firms for shipping law in the country. For weeks after she got her position, I heard my father tell his friends at church about her superior negotiating skills and enormous confidence. My mother told me that once, when Rania was a baby, my father heated her hairbrush in the microwave for a few seconds so that it wasn't too cold for her head. When I told my father that I wanted to study politics, a totally impractical subject, he gave me a solemn look, to which I responded, exhausted, 'I'm never going to be Rania.' He smiled at me that day — apparently, I said that to him a lot growing up — but despite his insistence that my sister and I were different and that it wasn't a competition, I never quite believed him.

'What do you want to be when you grow up?' Somehow the question was always more complicated for me than it was for Rania and Raf. Both got their jobs straight out of university without much fuss or lengthy discussion, my sister at a prestigious law firm and my brother in wealth management at a big American bank. I don't remember them ever wanting to do anything else. Those were their identities, and they made sense, safely positioning them on a straight path towards financial security.

By contrast, I was never sure what I wanted to be. I was curious and wanted to discover the world, much like my father when he decided to leave Egypt and move to a country he had barely visited. Both he and I are the youngest of our siblings; perhaps it's the prerogative of the last child to take chances and not to have to conform. Still, I didn't think I was truly free to do something different with my life.

I remember my primary school English teacher, a tall, elderly woman with impeccable posture called Mrs McCloud, telling me I could grow up to be whatever I wanted. She imparted this wisdom every weekday evening as she drove me from school back to Number 29, a convenient arrangement given she lived down the road. I never believed Mrs McCloud. It's not that I thought she was lying to me; she was particularly gentle and well intentioned. The kind of person who would gasp when she heard on the radio that there had been a murder and say, 'Why ever would someone do such a thing?'

Perhaps it was her innocent disposition that made me think Mrs McCloud just didn't notice that my family and I were different. When she dropped me off, all she saw was a large house on the corner of a lush London street. Based on that, she assumed that I had the resources to do whatever I wanted. She wasn't wrong. But most careers didn't feel like they were real options for me. It wasn't just about my brother and sister; all six of my uncles were engineers and doctors, and none of their wives worked. I had 25 first cousins, and every single one of them who worked was a doctor, lawyer, or — you guessed it — an engineer.

Watching my father build his career from scratch in a new

country instilled a strong work ethic in all three of us. Financial independence was encouraged in our house. From a young age, my father would let us earn our pocket money by doing chores around the house and clearing the garden. We would be given our earnings on our way to church every Sunday, so that we could spend it on chocolate from the corner shop after the service. No chores meant no chocolate, and there were no exceptions.

Although I always imagined I would work when I grew up, I never believed I could do anything outside of the few sanctioned careers. Not because I was ever told that, but because I'd never seen anyone in my family pursue other jobs, nor had I been exposed to the people who did. There were no journalists in my community; I'd never met one growing up. I liked watching and reading the news, but I saw myself as an observer of world events, not someone who'd ever experience them first-hand. The people who did that, the reporters on television, didn't have olive skin and curly black hair. Especially the few who were women. While I was growing up, the only woman of colour I remember seeing on the news was an anchor called Moira Stuart. She was serious but not afraid to show her character, smiling wryly at her guests when they said something she didn't agree with. Her elegant, upright posture exuded confidence. I loved watching her. Around the same time, I noticed another reporter called Lyse Doucet, who was reporting from the Middle East. She stood out to me because of her strong Canadian accent, which again was an anomaly for the BBC. I remember her calm and precise reporting from Jerusalem immediately following a suicide bombing, wondering how she could be so composed in such a dangerous moment.

I didn't know Moira or Lyse, but I imagined they had very different lives to mine. I bet they didn't live at home with their parents into their mid-20s or spend hours in the kitchen with their mothers every weekend, stuffing grape leaves with minced meat and spices. Journalists like them were tough and street-smart, I thought. I could barely navigate the manicured streets of North London alone, and I still blushed when I saw couples kissing in the park.

I wasn't journalism material, not a *halfie* like me.

2.

A Perfect Match

The first time I set foot in a newsroom was in the BBC headquarters in White City, London, the summer after the 9/11 attacks. I have a memory of flying paper and scattered worktables lying in the shadows of a manicured set, where perfectly made-up presenters sat at big desks, smiling into even bigger cameras. I was instantly drawn to the magnificent mess behind the scenes.

I was there as a pseudo-expert to advise one of the senior producers on a long-format piece they were running about the Middle East. By now, I had completed my undergraduate degree and was still living with my parents while undertaking a master's in Middle Eastern politics. I had become completely engrossed in the subject, and my parents encouraged my studies, despite the fact that they didn't seem to be leading to a career.

Learning about the Middle East wasn't just an academic pursuit for me. It connected me to my family and its past. I wrote my dissertation on Egypt during its socialist experiment in the 1950s and 1960s, a time when my mother had been forced to flee in the middle of the night after the government confiscated her father's properties and businesses, rendering them homeless. My father, too, had witnessed armed guards force their way into his home and confiscate the cotton factory my grandfather had spent his life building. The soldiers wouldn't even let his father go back upstairs to get his glasses. In large part, this period defined how my parents came to feel about Egypt, why they left, and why they never wanted to live there again.

Immediately after 9/11, I started writing policy briefs about Iraq and Al Qaeda for my academic supervisor. Suddenly, Arab experts were in high demand, and my obsession with the region was proving useful beyond the university circles I was used to. From the British foreign office to think tanks and newsrooms, I was invited to explain the politics and governmental structures in the Middle East to officials, experts, and journalists. I embraced using my historical knowledge to analyse the present moment, and relished being part of a growing conversation about combatting extremism in the Middle East. Questions about the strength of the terrorist group Al Qaeda, and how much of a global threat was Iraqi President Saddam Hussein, were key to determining what would happen next. These were tough and complicated issues, yet some politicians were rushing to answer them and making big errors in the process.

I ended up staying at the BBC for most of that day, silently watching from the corner of the newsroom as the journalists stood seriously in small circles with pens in their hands, discussing what to cover and how. Some of them had dark skin and brown eyes, but spoke with an English accent — *halfies*, I thought, just like me.

I heard the words 'axis of evil' a few times. It had been a few months since US President Bush had coined his famous sound bite, but it was still a major topic of conversation, including in the BBC newsroom. The US and its allies had invaded Afghanistan, and in Iraq Saddam Hussein had turned down another request from the UN for a weapons inspection. The Americans were making noises about another invasion. They were talking about how the entire region — *my* region — was alight.

On one of the big screens next to me, I saw an analyst discussing how it was likely that Saddam had weapons of mass destruction, and the merits of going to war. At one point, one of the producers in the circle ran over to his desk, picked up the phone, and instructed the director to play 'street pictures of Baghdad' over the voice of the analyst. While he spoke about war and destruction, the viewers could see the faces of the people who would bear the brunt of it. Ordinary people, walking, shopping, smiling. Children playing, an old man selling bread.

It struck me that these journalists were deciding not only which information people were receiving, but also controlling how that information was consumed. It was as if someone had let me in on a secret — my understanding of the world around me was shaped by these people, the people who processed events and reported them to everyone else. They made decisions that influenced my thoughts and opinions, and thus to some extent my actions, as well as everyone else's. The news didn't just happen, it was *made* — and it was the journalists in this newsroom who did that. *What enormous responsibility these people have*, I thought.

What an opportunity, not just to witness the suffering and injustice happening right now, but to alert the rest of the world, to do something about it.

It was in that moment, sitting quietly in a newsroom, that journalism found me. Or maybe it was the other way around. Like many love affairs, it's hard to say for sure who instigated it.

I went home after my visit to the BBC and announced to my parents that I was going to be a reporter — it was the perfect job for me given my passion for the region, its people, and the events that were unfolding. I described the newsroom — the giant cameras and the words scrolling inside the teleprompters, clever people sitting at messy desks covered in half-filled cups of coffee. My father asked me a few questions, but said very little. He was still eating his dinner, slowly taking the skin off his roast chicken, dipping it into garlicky yoghurt, and placing the chunks in his mouth.

My mother was cleaning the stove, carefully taking off the burners with rubber gloves so that she could clean underneath them, thick suds coating the surface. She seemed engrossed in the task, but I knew she was listening; I could see her smiling when I got animated.

Ideas like these were usually met with vague amusement from my parents. In fact, I don't remember them ever saying no or forbidding me to do anything; they would just stay quiet until the idea passed. At times, I felt that they were proud of my sense of adventure, or at least my father was. But it was often hard to reconcile their encouragement of me to pursue my own path with their instinct to protect me and keep me close.

When I was choosing which university to attend, I had picked one that was outside London, which would have meant moving out of Number 29. My parents barely said anything about it at the time, but I overheard my mother on the phone saying how worried she was that I would be moving away, questioning whether I was ready. Once, I heard her crying to my father about it, and even wondered whether she meant for me to overhear. Neither my sister nor my brother had left home until they got married.

I was upset with her for not trusting me, but I eventually stayed at home anyway after not getting good enough grades for my first-choice university. I believe they would have let me go had I got in, but I would have felt guilty for leaving. Now, I was proposing another adventurous plan that would take me far away from them, but they probably didn't believe it would ever really happen.

'So, what do you think about me becoming a journalist?' I finally asked them.

'*Insha'Allah*,' my father replied, not paying much attention and getting back to his plate.

———

I can't blame my parents for not taking me seriously. Journalism wasn't the first career I had got excited about. There was a time when I wanted to be a teacher, then a doctor, and then — for an entire summer — a hotel caterer, despite having shown no previous interest in food, let alone cooking. My mother sometimes indulged these fantasies. She had even taken me to a Swiss catering company in London to find out which qualifications I would need.

But in journalism I found a home for my interests, a place
where they had the potential to make a difference. As the
American-led invasion of Iraq progressed, I started to watch the
news differently, noticing how my opinions and my mood as a
viewer were swayed by the images and commentary. I didn't always
agree with it — there was a hysteria and anger in the coverage
that penetrated every conversation and flattened perceptions.
Rigorous journalism was increasingly taking a back seat to
accommodate the need for stories that fitted a certain narrative.
It didn't seem like it took much, or even any, evidence to trace
a 'link' between a particular country and Al Qaeda. Across the
Muslim world, these links — although often based on nothing —
were made so frequently it started to create the false image that
many of these countries were filled with little else but extremists.

I began applying for jobs in television news, starting with the
bigger networks. I quickly realised why I had never before considered journalism as a career option, and why my family had not
taken my ambitions seriously. British mainstream media in the
early 2000s was as unaccepting of outsiders as the other cultural
industries, particularly when it came to hiring journalists, and
certainly when it came to deciding who to put on their screens.

I made it to the last round of interviews for a BBC trainee
position that was known as one of the best and most competitive
entry-level roles at the organisation. One afternoon, I got a call
from a BBC producer who introduced herself as one of the women
on my interview panel. She explained that I had answered their
questions well but that I had not got the position. I had come
in second place and, apparently, should be very proud of myself
for making it that far. When I asked for feedback, she hesitated,

finally admitting to me that the panel had had an issue with my accent. She explained that I rolled my 'R's and so it was hard to understand everything I was saying.

'It's really not your fault,' she insisted, and went on to recount how she had once taken a trip to the Pyramids in Egypt and really enjoyed it. I stopped her; I wanted to make sure she knew I was born in London and had grown up there. Nobody had ever, *ever* said that my English was hard to understand. If anything, I was aware that to lots of people I probably sounded quite posh. How could I lose out on a job because of an accent I never knew I had? But the more I explained my background, the more uncomfortable she became, until eventually she made an excuse and hung up.

Not long afterwards, I managed to get a short, unpaid internship with another British channel in their office near the Houses of Parliament. My job consisted of intercepting guests who were in the building to appear on other networks and luring them to the ITV studios. After I had spent a month diligently spotting, convincing, and guiding members of parliament, analysts, and once even the British foreign secretary on to ITV's screens, the show's editor commended me on my powers of persuasion. I told him I wanted to become a reporter doing hard-hitting interviews one day, at which point he burst out laughing.

'You're far too *exotic* for British television, my dear — look at you! And your name is *Shay-reen Tafros,* for God's sake!' he said. 'I would stick to jobs behind the camera, if I were you. Have you ever considered becoming a local fixer, or even a translator?'

After months of searching, I got a job helping out at a Saudi-owned Arabic-language news station called Al Arabiya. It wasn't quite a job because again I was working for free — or 'training', as they called it. The industry was so competitive that even unpaid positions were hard to find. I was living at home with my parents supporting me, and so, unlike many others just starting out, I was able to accept these internships without thinking twice, in the hope they would lead to a paid position in time. My new role involved booking guests to speak on various topics and setting up stories for the London bureau chief, a chain-smoking Lebanese reporter with razor-sharp instincts named Mohamed Chebaro.

I turned up before anyone else every morning and made sure I was always the last one to leave the office. I developed a simple system to book guests and organise their taxis to and from the studio, which was my only real role, and uploaded all the bureau contacts to an online database that I got a friend to design for free.

But my efforts were hardly noticed. Or maybe they were, but it still didn't make a difference. My spoken Arabic wasn't strong enough for broadcast, and my reading was too slow to be useful for fixing or advising on Mohamed's scripts. I was frustrated and disillusioned, and I didn't want to continue working for the network for another reason: Al Arabiya was perceived by many as a propaganda tool for the Saudi government. In the summer of 2005, while I was working there, the Saudi ruler, King Fahd, died, and it was the only story we were allowed to cover for the following three days. I was under strict instructions to vet our guests to make sure they only had favourable things to say about the ruler. A few months into the traineeship, I decided that if I had to work for an Arab channel, there was only one I was interested in.

Like other Arab kids my age, Al Jazeera's opening jingle was the soundtrack to my teenage years. I hummed it on the way to university, while I was doing coursework, in the shower. I must have heard that five-second melody dozens of times a day, and it had etched itself into my unconscious. It would play in my mind's ear even when the television was on mute; just the image of a news presenter smiling and mouthing, '*Marhaba*,' — 'Welcome' — the huge gold calligraphy of the Al Jazeera logo twirling to reveal itself, was enough to set it jangling in my brain.

Launched in 1996, Al Jazeera had become one of the five most influential brands in the world — up there with Apple, Starbucks, and Google. The Qatari-owned network had tens of millions of viewers across the Arabic-speaking world, far more than any other pan-Arab channel. It was known for its hard-hitting, controversial style of news-making. Its slogan, 'The opinion and the other opinion', signalled a commitment to bringing all sides and points of view to the table, including booking Israeli guests speaking in Hebrew — unheard of for Arab channels at the time, which were largely tools of state propaganda. It was also controversial abroad, especially after the 9/11 attacks, when it started to air videos of Osama bin Laden it had obtained through Al Qaeda. The channel was heavily criticised for giving the group a platform to spew its hateful rhetoric, but Al Jazeera argued that the tapes were newsworthy and any other network would have done the same if they had been given them.

Al Jazeera was a phenomenon, changing the rules of journalism in the Arab world. It revelled in the near-accurate perception of itself as hated by governments and loved by the people. Other networks were both in awe of and highly frustrated by the unruly style of Al Jazeera, which depended on local sources and domestic reporters more than talent flown in from abroad. Its mission statement was to 'spread an understanding of democracy and human rights', especially in the Arab world, according to the head of the network at the time, Wadah Khanfar.

Wadah was one of those people whose personality doesn't match their looks. He was short and stocky, with round eyes and floppy hair. But when he spoke, the room went quiet. Every word was meticulously selected for maximum impact. At once a hustler and an intellectual, he had risen up the chain of command through sheer hard work. His first jobs at the network had been as a driver and then a reporter in the mid-1990s. He had ascended in the scrappy and chaotic environment that defined how Al Jazeera operated, and in overseeing its rise he had become a legend in the industry.

While I was still working at Al Arabiya, rumours began circulating that Al Jazeera was going to launch an English-language channel, called Al Jazeera English, and that its headquarters would be in Qatar with offices all around the world.

The rumours were true, and Mohamed Chebaro had given me a heads-up about the opportunity. 'You would be a perfect match for them; they're looking for Arab talent. Or, even, Arab *lite*,' he chuckled, winking at me as if I knew exactly what he was talking about.

I ignored the jibe, which I guessed was a reference to the fact that I had never lived in the Middle East. I had not really thought of myself as 'Arab talent' before. In fact, I wasn't sure which part of the description fit less — me being an Arab or being talented.

But I instantly connected with the idea of an Al Jazeera channel in English. Proudly headquartered in the Middle East, it would be geared towards English speakers thirsty for another perspective on the news. At Al Jazeera, my divided identity — Arab and yet also British — would finally be an asset. I instantly started getting excited at the prospect of joining the new channel, which was planning to build a big broadcast hub in London, not far from Number 29.

After a series of interviews over the course of several months, I finally got a call back, just as I was giving up. I was sitting at my desk at Al Arabiya, logging an interview Mohamed had just done with a counter-terrorism expert, when I ran to the bathroom and sat down on a closed toilet seat to take the call.

'Hello?' I offered, trying not to sound breathless, and unhelpfully channelling all my nervous energy into gripping the flush handle with my left hand.

'Hi, Sherine. It's Jo Bergen from Al Jazeera English. I'm calling to give you good news!'

I imagined Jo sitting at her desk, a list of names and numbers in front of her, making dozens of these calls, mostly disappointing people. She was probably almost as relieved as I was about this one.

'We would love for you to come and work for us in our London office,' she continued, pausing to allow the information to sink in.

'Okay, thank you for letting me know,' I responded, as if Jo had just confirmed my restaurant reservation.

I had discussed this moment several times with my father, and he had instructed me to stay calm and not accept anything until I saw the package they were offering. '*When* you get the job, *insha'Allah* ...' he would begin, at which I would smile coyly at how confident he was in me, despite his initial silence about my chosen career path.

I hung up the phone. Jo promised to send the job offer via email by the end of the day. I didn't care how much money they were offering — that was the only good thing about working for free; everything from here was a pay rise. I was about to be part of something monumental, the launch of a channel that would change the course of television news. An outlet for stories from all over the world that otherwise would never be told.

I could hear the jingle in my head again and decided to let it out this time, still sitting on the toilet lid and gripping the flush as I sang.

———

Al Jazeera English is what happens when you start a news channel with a blank cheque. In those early days, there was no story too expensive, no salary too high. In the months before the launch of the channel, dozens of reporters were sent all over the world to film stories just for practice and to collect file footage and stories for the shelves. That meant there was a trove of backup feature pieces for slow news days when we needed to fill the bulletins. Naturally, the majority of these stories were never aired, because by the time we launched they were out of date. Even I, the most junior person in the building, was allowed to produce a story I had pitched on fish smuggling in the Canary Islands. I spent days on a Greenpeace boat looking for smugglers and eventually did some secret filming in the port, where I caught them in action. Unfortunately, the police saw us on the security cameras, and the next day we were told to leave Las Palmas. The story cost over $10,000, and it never aired. I'm pretty sure I'm still not welcome back on the island.

My first role in the London office was as one of three researchers. There, I did everything from photocopying scripts and carrying tapes, to collecting information and making calls. In a newsroom of dozens of journalists, the researchers were paid the least, and producers often got us to do menial tasks they didn't feel like doing.

Despite the fact that our launch kept being delayed, there was excitement among the staff. Many of the reporters came from British networks, like the BBC and Channel 4. Some were heavy hitters in journalism, like Sir David Frost, who became legendary after a series of iconic interviews with former US president Richard Nixon and went on to present the BBC's flagship Sunday breakfast show for many years. I had grown up watching Frost on television as he interviewed political figures from all over the world, and now here he was in our newsroom, casually walking by my desk and saying, 'Good morning,' every day, as if we were old colleagues. He'd even make jokes sometimes about how well staffed the office was for a station that wasn't yet on air. 'He's a comedian, you know, as well as one of the most famous hosts on British television,' a colleague informed me once.

The producers and I would sit around edit suites discussing why we had joined the channel and how Al Jazeera English was going to be different: invested in showing the nuance of events and offering a platform to marginalised voices. Where other channels had lost their way, sensationalising the news and making it about the reporter, we were going to bring the story back to the people. The desire to band together to make the channel a success was infectious. I'd not felt anything like it before.

The premise of the channel was simple enough — AJE, as it

came to be known, wanted to be the first truly global news channel. There would be no such thing as a *foreign* story; all stories
would be covered by local reporters who spoke the language, or
at the very least lived in the countries they were covering. AJE's
philosophy was the antithesis to so-called 'parachute journalism',
when reporters are dropped into different countries to report on
breaking news stories.

The channel had four broadcast centres — the main hub in
Doha, Qatar, in addition to ones in Kuala Lumpur, London, and
Washington, DC — each in a prestigious location. In London,
that meant a luxurious building at No. 1 Grosvenor Square, near
Park Lane. It was the place on the Monopoly board that you
never wanted to land on, because staying at a hotel there meant
bankruptcy.

After only a few months of working in the London office,
my boss asked me to move to the Qatari hub in Doha to see how
I would perform as a junior producer and reporter. Just as my
former boss Mohamed Chebaro had predicted, the channel had
a bias in favour of Middle Easterners with British accents. For
my new, and predominantly white, British bosses, I was the breed
of correspondent they were looking for. I had the right look but
also the right ethos: I was just as committed as they were to lofty
notions of fairness and balance in reporting.

I had no doubt that moving to Doha was the right career
decision. It was a huge leap towards becoming a reporter, and
the channel still hadn't even launched. For those reasons, my
father was supportive of the move, even though it represented a
complete break from my life up to that point. Leaving my parents
and the comfortable confines of Number 29, the only home I had

ever known, made me more anxious than I was willing to admit. No more Saturday games in the park with my brother, no more church on Sundays followed by long family lunches. I was abandoning the routines and rituals that shaped my small, safe world.

There had been moments growing up when I had rebelled against this world, questioning my parents as to why I had to spend Sunday mornings at church while the rest of my friends were having a lie-in. But those moments were short-lived, and for the most part I appreciated the comfort of my life, and knew what I was risking by leaving. The consolation was that it was only a trial period. If I didn't like living in Doha after six months, or if I felt homesick, then my boss assured me I could return to London and negotiate a new contract.

I flew to Doha a few days after my 26th birthday. My parents took me to Heathrow airport, staying with me until the last possible moment. The only time I had travelled without them before was when I had gone to Australia with my childhood friend Yosra before starting my master's. They had taken me to the airport that day, too, my mother asking a stream of questions about whether I had packed enough sunscreen and stuffing my carry-on with granola bars. This time, though, it felt different as I kissed them goodbye. There were no questions, no need to ask if I had packed enough of anything, because there was no certainty of when I was going to return.

As I was taking my shoes off to place in the X-ray machine, I looked back at my parents, who were still standing by the security cordon, despite the fact that I was already out of their line of sight. I saw my mother's face buried in my father's shoulder, the patch of light-blue shirt beneath her head darkening from the tears. He stroked her hair softly and whispered something in her ear. I knew what he was saying: 'God is with her.'

They were worried — I was really leaving this time; it wasn't just another one of my ideas that they could keep quiet about until it passed. But I also knew they were proud of me for being brave enough to leave home and seek a new adventure. Just like they had done.

———

Following several weeks of technical delays, Al Jazeera English launched on 15 November 2006. The mood in the newsroom in Doha that morning was a combination of nauseous anxiety and excited anticipation. It wasn't just the obscene amount of Qatari money it had taken to get the channel up and running. The careers of dozens of journalists were on the line, well-known reporters who had gambled on the unknown by leaving their jobs at established broadcasters like CNN, the BBC, and PBS.

The newsroom was a spectacular structure: a huge circular space, largely taken up by a presenters' desk and the long virtual wall behind it. Tied to the ceiling were rows and rows of lights in different colours and sizes, with thick silver chains holding them all together. Thousands of coloured wires stretched across the ceiling, snaking all the way around the newsroom, each one responsible for transmitting picture or sound. The desks, the chairs, the lights — everything was brand new.

The first broadcast had to be perfect, which meant that we had pre-recorded several segments for the first hour of the 'live' show. I was watching, unnoticed, from the top floor of the newsroom, close to the anchor's desk. I hadn't been assigned to do anything. That day, even the most senior producers, who had previously written and directed award-winning documentaries, were reduced to writing basic lines for the presenters.

Director Wadah Khanfar walked into the centre of the newsroom and stood by the senior editors on an elevated section. The room fell silent as he leaned on a desk, smiling as if he was enjoying every second of this moment. It wasn't often that you would see Wadah around the newsroom, although his presence seemed always to be floating over us, like a news god silently directing us. With his usual down-to-earth brand of charisma, Wadah congratulated us on the launch and told us that we would each remember this day as the start of something new — a chance to give a 'voice to the voiceless' and make a difference. Listening to him, I had the feeling that I was exactly where I needed to be.

After he was done, we took our places and the camera lights switched on — it was time. The music started, that familiar tune which now filled my insides with nervous energy and pride. 'It's November the fifteenth, day one of a new era of television news,' announced Sami Zeidan, the news presenter, to the viewers — as the entire newsroom held its breath. We were broadcasting to over 80 million cable and satellite viewers across the world.

'CUT,' yelled the director. Everyone stopped. Before I realised what was happening, a floor manager had taken me by the arm and I was being instructed to go and get my make-up done.

'But why? Why? What do they want me to do?' I kept asking the make-up artist in a panic, as the buzz of the airbrush spat concealer at me so fast it felt like tiny needles were puncturing my cheeks. I was told not to worry; they just wanted some people to sit and look like they were working while the camera panned the newsroom. 'You know,' the make-up artist said, 'like an extra in a movie.'

It took less than ten minutes to get my face made up and hair ready. I finished and grabbed my phone to message my mother about my new role in the upcoming bulletin. Just then, I caught a glimpse of myself in the mirror — what was the point of telling her, I thought; she wouldn't even recognise me under all the dark eyeshadow and fake lashes that had been applied to my face.

Moments later, we filmed the opening sequence again. This time it worked. The director declared it a success, and I became an immovable part of Al Jazeera's story and of television news history, sitting there in the background, wearing my new eyes and pretending to type.

3.

Counterflow

The novelty of working in a newsroom had started to wear off by my sixth straight day of ten-hour shifts. My role mainly involved watching images coming in from our teams on the ground and writing scripts using information gathered from news wires. Long hours passed in which I'd sit trying to look important with nothing much to do, punctured by moments of intense excitement when there was breaking news.

The main launch story for AJE was the growing political tension in Lebanon. Hezbollah, a Shi'a Muslim group and political party backed by Syria and Iran, was leading a campaign against the Lebanese prime minister Fouad Siniora's anti-Syrian cabinet. Hezbollah's popularity had soared after they'd claimed victory over Israel during the Lebanon War in 2006. The group felt emboldened and was quickly absorbed into Siniora's new coalition government, becoming part of the ruling authority for the first time. But it wasn't enough for them, and a power struggle ensued. Hezbollah's representative quit after the prime minister rejected their demand for veto power on government decisions. In December 2006, thousands of opposition supporters staged a sit-in in downtown Beirut, vowing to stay until the government resigned.

I jumped at the first chance to go to Lebanon to help cover the unfolding crisis. I had fond memories of Lebanon, especially Beirut. My parents would take me and my siblings there, usually during the Christmas break, on our way to Egypt, just for fun and to visit friends. It was a vibrant, free city where I was allowed to wear what I wanted, and nobody looked at me disapprovingly or made nasty comments like they did in Cairo. At least not in the areas I visited. The best thing about Beirut was the beauty salons. They were everywhere, on every corner, like Starbucks in New York. In busy shopping areas, you could find several salons within a one-mile stretch. My mother would take me and my sister to one downtown, the same salon that her mother had taken her to when she was a girl. When we walked in, the ritual conversation would begin — the big smiles and welcome, the questions about my grandmother, a teasing comment about my mother's fluctuating weight, and then a list of all the things that had gone wrong in the country since they had seen her last. I couldn't always understand what the women in the salon were saying, because I wasn't used to the Lebanese dialect, but everyone spoke the universal language of beauty: 'highlight', 'lowlight', 'cut', 'threading' were the English words, and then you had the French ones, '*leese*' (if you wanted your hair blow-dried straight) and '*quaret*' (if you wanted it cut short, with no layers). I learned these terms proudly, as if I was learning a secret language to which only women in the Middle East were privy.

Once you walked into a Beirut salon, you surrendered yourself (and every hair on your body) to the beauticians. The very first time I went to get my eyebrows threaded, aged thirteen, I left the room with dark-brown tinted brows and fake eyelashes. The lady didn't ask if I wanted it done; she just went ahead, casually telling me what she was doing as if alerting me that she was removing something stuck in my teeth. Luckily, I was able to stop her before she injected something into my lips that she claimed was 'just to poof them up a little'.

My father, meanwhile, waited for us in a coffee shop on the high street, sipping a vanilla latte, which came with cinnamon sprinkled on top in the shape of a cedar tree, like the Lebanese flag. The other cities in the Middle East where I spent time growing up often felt like they were desperate to conform to a Western idea of sophistication. Restaurants offered burgers and spaghetti bolognese instead of local food, and the only thing to drink was Pepsi or 'Coke Cola'. In Beirut, though, we always ate Lebanese food, sitting for hours after we'd finished, watching my father smoke his smouldering shisha pipe packed with mint and lemon-flavoured tobacco.

I never minded the long, narrow roads our taxi drivers angrily navigated, or spending hours in traffic getting back to our hotel. It was common for the residents to complain about the weak internet and frequent blackouts, which were unsurprising given the state of the power lines that hung off half-destroyed buildings. As a tourist, though, these were just eccentricities. I loved sitting by the sea, watching groups of elderly women power-walking down the corniche, wearing full make-up. I remember the first time I noticed the buildings with bullet holes in their exteriors, and my father explaining about the 15-year civil war that had ended in 1990. Over 120,000 people had been killed, and many more fled the country. I wondered if the houses had been left like that on purpose to remind the Lebanese of the destruction that happens when neighbours turn on each other.

By early 2007, when I started going there for work, Beirut still felt like a serious city, but it had a cool vibe, its creativity still in evidence despite its troubled past. My deployments to the Beirut bureau were easy. I spent a couple of weeks there each time, answering the phones, booking guests, and helping out with logistics. In the afternoons, I strolled through town, speaking to people in the cafes and protest tents about what was happening, slowly gaining a better understanding of why they were so angry with Siniora's government. I was fascinated by how popular Hezbollah had become, going from an outcast guerrilla group in the 1980s to a major political and military force after the war with Israel in 2006. Hezbollah appealed not just to Shi'a Muslims but also to the Christian sects. At first, I assumed this was an alliance of convenience against the government, but as I spoke to the protestors it became clear that they saw Hezbollah, and its leader, Hassan Nasrallah, as the strongest and most legitimate force in the country. Hezbollah's logo – an arm reaching out of one of the letters in the organisation's name, holding up an assault rifle – was emblazoned on flags and yellow T-shirts that had somehow come to symbolise rejection of government corruption and support for the will of the people within an increasingly fragile state.

I quickly discovered that I could happily spend hours sitting with people discussing politics and asking them questions. I much preferred being out on the streets to being in the office. It was as if the books I had read at university, with their theories of how sociopolitical structures formed in the region, were now coming to life. It helped that I could converse in Arabic, and I discovered that my Anglo-Egyptian accent was an icebreaker rather than an impediment.

Beirut was sometimes tense, and there was sporadic fighting, but I didn't witness any of the violence at first. Then, in the first week of May 2008, the situation escalated after the government declared Hezbollah's elaborate communications network an attack on state sovereignty. It accused the group of spying, and fired an important Hezbollah ally from a key position. Street battles suddenly broke out across the country between Hezbollah and pro-government forces. Dread about a repeat of Lebanon's bloody civil war was growing, not just among analysts but among the Lebanese people. Violence became so intense that Beirut's airport was shut down, along with government buildings and commercial businesses.

I was in Doha at the time, and the only way to get to Beirut was to fly to the Syrian capital of Damascus. With my Egyptian passport, it would be easy to get into Syria without a visa. From there, I would drive across the border with Lebanon, a journey I volunteered to make. Over the past eighteen months in Beirut, I had witnessed the indifference of people on the street turn into anger and then rage, wondering every time whether this would be the moment it exploded. I was eager to see for myself what was happening, and to reconnect with the protestors I had met. I wasn't worried about the violence; to the contrary, I felt invincible: a privilege of the young, hungry, and inexperienced.

On the way to the airport, I called my mother, reassuring her that this was just another assignment and promising to text as soon as I arrived. We had made a deal before my first deployment: I promised always to respond to her messages, even if just with a word or a letter, so that she would know I was safe. It was the only way we had found to cope with her anxiety over me being sent to a place that could turn into a war zone at any moment. This was a situation she and my father could never have imagined. Yet despite their doubts, they had been by my side on my journey to become a journalist, encouraging me after each rejection and acting as my biggest supporters. Now I was on the cusp of making it, and the reality of my unconventional choice of career was setting in.

———

The plane to Damascus was still in mid-air when, disregarding the pleas of flight attendants, the passengers started getting up and opening the overhead compartments, a not-uncommon scene on journeys to the Middle East. I'm not sure where the lack of patience comes from. Passengers who have spent half the day on a plane, happily watching their movies and eating, suddenly decide — several minutes before landing — that they *must* get their bags and head for the exit before everyone else, as though otherwise they could miss their stop.

By the time the seat belt sign dimmed, everyone on the plane was standing in the aisles, shuffling and stretching their limbs. I was still in my seat, in no hurry to leave. Even though it had only

been a few months since my last deployment there, it was starting to sink in that this was not going to be the Lebanon I knew. I
was getting nervous: not only was it my first major breaking news
story, it was the channel's, too. My instructions were clear — to
get into the country and help out in our Beirut office, as I had
done before, but I'd be doing it in a very different atmosphere
this time.

I made it through passport control and headed for the taxi
rank outside the airport to look for someone to take me across the
Syrian–Lebanese border. It was a tall ask, and I didn't have much
time; the sun was starting to rise. In the few hours between being
deployed and catching my flight, I had spoken on the phone to
our Beirut correspondent, Rula Amin. She had previously worked
for CNN, where she had been first to break the news of the death
of the Syrian president Hafez al-Assad in 2000 and report on
the Israeli disengagement from Gaza in 2005. I had watched her
before on television, poised and confident in designer shirts, her
wild auburn hair brushing her shoulders.

During my trips to Lebanon, Rula had become a friend as
well as a mentor, teaching me how to cultivate contacts, from
government officials to the inner circle of Hezbollah. Rula pos-
sessed that rare ability to be respected and taken seriously by all
sides involved in the conflict. When I asked her how she did it,
her advice was simple: take the time to seek out, understand,
and explain to the viewers the strongest argument that each side
presents, whatever that may be. If you do that well, nobody will
accuse you of being biased. Rula also went shopping with me to
buy tops that suited my skin tone, and taught me how to tame
my frizzy hair in case I was ever on air. She let me in on the

secret to looking good on television. 'Lighting, my dear,' she said. 'Everything else is extra.'

When I called her from Damascus airport, she warned me that the situation in Beirut was worsening and instructed me to head straight to the border before it got too crazy.

I found Abu Tarek in front of the airport exit. He was standing by his car with one leg still in the vehicle and both arms slumped over the roof. It reminded me of the way my father stood when we got stuck in heavy Cairo traffic, peering out to see where the blockage was. There were two other cars parked behind with similar-looking men inside. Apart from that, there was nobody else around; the city was still asleep.

Abu Tarek's face was painfully dry, tight, and tanned. His lips were cracked, and flakes of skin had found their way into his thick beard. Despite the cold morning air, he wasn't wearing a coat, just layers of clothes that looked old and stained. As soon as I approached him, our eyes locked and he smiled widely, revealing a mouth of crooked teeth. Millions of tiny wrinkles appeared as he scrunched his face, trying to work out what my deal was — young and well dressed, face made up. Most likely he decided I was in Damascus for fun or to see family.

'How much to take me to Beirut?' I asked in Arabic, quickly and confidently so that he didn't get a chance to detect my accent.

Abu Tarek's smile vanished. This wasn't the interaction he had expected. He raised his eyebrows and took his foot out of the car, getting close to me.

'It's dangerous to go to the border right now,' he replied, as he fumbled in his pocket and took out a pack of Marlboro Reds. 'I don't know.'

I watched him carefully but didn't respond. After a few seconds, I turned to leave, wheeling my baggage around behind me in an exaggerated loop.

'Wait, okay. Four hundred dollars,' he said loudly. I couldn't quite work out if it was a question or a statement.

I shook my head and continued to walk away from him. We had begun the familiar souk-style negotiation, and I knew we had one more round to go.

'Okay, three hundred. I can take you to the Masnaa crossing; I don't know what will happen after that,' he said, reaching out for my luggage as if this was a great deal and there was no way I would counter. Three hundred dollars was a lot more than it normally cost. But then again, these were not normal times.

I got in the car as he mumbled something about not even knowing if we could get across the border at a time like this. Finally, he turned the key in the ignition — once, twice, three times until the car started. He took a long drag of his cigarette before throwing it out of the window, turning back to me begrudgingly and saying, '*Yalla, mademoiselle*, let's go to the border if that's what you want from me,' as if I were the one taking advantage of the situation, and not the other way around.

Just over an hour later, the grassy farmlands of Lebanon's Bekaa Valley started to appear in the distance, north of where we were heading. The border crossing was swarming with cars.

'Ahh, this is too much, even for Masnaa,' remarked Abu Tarek, sounding more tired than concerned. He was referring to the Masnaa Border Crossing, which is one of three corridors between Syria and Lebanon, and the primary one that connects the capitals. While the other two are mainly used for cargo,

Masnaa has a separate lane for private cars and is the border of choice for individuals travelling between the two countries, as well as for smugglers for whom small bribes go a long way.

As we got closer, I could see what looked like hundreds of coaches, cars, and buses, scattered unapologetically around makeshift checkpoints along the narrow road.

'It just opened, that's why it's so busy — let's go and have some tea and come back later,' Abu Tarek suggested. I got out of the car and ran to a high point to get a better look at what was happening on the other side of the crossing. It was clear the chaos wasn't just a result of the early morning rush hour.

People were fleeing Lebanon with all their belongings — suit-cases bulging at the seams, most of them not even fully closed. One woman was carrying an ironing board in one arm, a small child in the other, weaving around the cars to get to the front. Some had abandoned their cars on the highway, others looked like they had been walking for many miles. People were shouting, fighting in the queue about who was there first, who was more desperate to get across the border. Mothers were trying to com-fort screaming children by the side of the road. These families had been forced to leave their homes and had no idea how long it would be before they could return, if ever.

I recalled the feeling I'd had the first time I saw masses of people amid the dirt and dust in Cairo's Garbage City. The way I had tried to help by giving stuff out with one hand and covering my nose with the other to counter the pungent smell of rot. I suddenly remembered how useless I had felt back then.

I was a spectator to the worst hours of these people's lives, and I suddenly felt angry that in other parts of the world, people were unaware, going about their days as they always did — at school, in cafes, watching movies — oblivious to the unfolding disaster. This time, though, I could do something. It was my job to tell people what was happening and make them care. This time, I thought, I would not walk away.

I took out my phone and started filming the crowds of people walking towards me. Most of them were so determined to reach the other side of the crossing that they didn't even notice me. The closer I got to the border, the more desperate the scenes became. I kept walking, trying to capture the chaos while weaving through the women and children. A few of them stopped to ask what I was doing. 'Just filming what's happening,' I replied. One of the few men told me he had been walking for hours and wasn't sure where the rest of his family were; they had separated when he had gone to find water. He warned me not to go any further because the clashes near the border were getting worse.

Before I knew it, I was at the checkpoint where the soldiers were, battling against the crowds coming my way. It was then that I realised how strange it was that I was heading in that direction. I was unconsciously being drawn towards the conflict, overriding my natural instinct to seek safety, and yet it felt right, unquestionably. I didn't feel useless or guilty anymore. Recording the people fleeing and telling their stories was the only thing that made sense to me in the moment. The only way, I thought, of finding some justice in this crazy situation.

'Miss Sherine!' shouted Abu Tarek, who was standing a few metres away waving his arms at me. I turned around and walked towards him, and he escorted me back to the car.

'It's not too much further now,' he said, battling once again with the ignition.

I didn't respond; I was still filming out of the window. An old woman with no shoes was sitting down in the dirt, holding a small baby in one arm. She looked up at me and blinked slowly, and then closed her eyes as if she had expended her last bit of energy.

After a few minutes, I put my phone away and noticed Abu Tarek was staring at me in the rear-view mirror. He looked confused, or maybe amused? It was hard to tell with all the lines on his face.

'Miss Sherine, sorry for asking, but what is a girl like you doing here?' he finally said.

I stared out of the window, telling myself not to be scared, that we were getting close and that my father would be proud of me. 'God is with you,' he would tell me, 'the angels will protect you.'

'The same as you, Abu Tarek. My job,' I replied, starting to believe it myself.

4.

Beirut Blunder

By the time I got to Beirut, the city was an intricate labyrinth of yellow-and-brown camouflaged vehicles: the sad sight of a city that had turned on itself. The army was deployed on the streets, and soldiers were everywhere — at checkpoints, traffic lights, the entrances to banks and state buildings. The authorities wanted to give the impression that the situation was under control. The Lebanese weren't buying it.

One of the less mundane tasks I was given by the Beirut team was to collect 'vox pops', opinions from ordinary Lebanese. I took the cameraman to a busy area and stopped people in the street to ask them what they thought of the situation.

In other cities, vox pops are a pain. When I was working at Al Arabiya in London, Mohamed Chebaro used to make me do them all the time. The topics ranged from 'What do you think of the prime minister?' to 'Do you think this city is dog-friendly?' Most of the time, nobody wanted to talk to you, and those few who did either answered with one word — 'Yes' — or two — 'Yes, probably' — or else went into a long rant about an entirely different subject.

But in Beirut, people were used to the press because of the large number of local news channels. They were usually happy to tell you what they thought of the situation. I was glad to have a chance to go out and speak to people again.

The story was complex and intimidating to report. There were different groups and sects allied with multiple regional players, and it was impossible to keep track. As my colleague Rula Amin had predicted, the clashes between Hezbollah and pro-government forces had intensified; they were the worst since the 1975–90 civil war. Heavily armed Hezbollah fighters had taken over much of western Beirut, vowing not to back down until the government conceded to the organisation's demands for more power in the cabinet. A proxy war had erupted between Hezbollah's supporters, Iran and Syria, on the one hand, and pro-government forces, backed by the US and Saudi Arabia, on the other. The violence was seen as a warning from Iran and Syria to US President Bush to stop interfering in the region. The prime minister and other prominent officials were holed up in their compounds, appealing to their Western allies for help in fighting what they called an 'armed coup' against Lebanon's democratic system. By the end of my first week in Beirut, the battles had killed over a dozen people and spread to the Bekaa Valley, northern Lebanon, and the Chouf Mountains.

In between my shifts at the bureau, I walked the nearby streets. Despite the risk of sporadic fighting, there were people milling around or sitting outside coffee shops, smoking shishas and working on their laptops. They weren't ignoring the violence so much as trying to function around it — as if the clashes were a series of road closures and all that was required was rerouting. Still, the city had changed — people weren't smiling, and I didn't hear the excited chatter of happy customers when I walked past the hairdressing or nail salons. Beirut felt heavy with dread and anticipation, bearing the weight of the entire region's political instability.

On the fourth day, there was a lull in the fighting. I had walked back to my hotel from the office slowly that evening, even stopping at some of the shops and trying on clothes I didn't need. It felt good to do something normal. By the time I got to my room, the sun had set, just in time for my ritual — bath, room service, romcom on the television, and, of course, the nightly phone call with my mother. I told her about my day and she listened, more interested in what I was eating and where I was going than my analysis of the political situation. I imagined her sitting at her dressing table while she spoke to me, meticulously applying her expensive night creams in the mirror. That evening, I fell asleep while she was still on the phone.

I slept through the first round of gunfire; the second one was more intense. It took me a few seconds to remember where I was and what I was doing there. On the television, Meg Ryan was on a train with a youthful Kevin Kline. The phone rang, and I found it buried in the thick duvet and answered. It was a producer from work, Amal Hamdan.

'Are you okay?' she asked urgently. She told me that gunfire had broken out near my hotel, outside the residence of a prominent politician and leader of the Future Movement party, Saad al-Hariri.

'You're the closest one to the office; you need to get there now. Doha want a live cross on what's happening,' she said without taking a breath.

I stayed silent, starting to feel nauseous and dizzy. I had never done a live cross, the term in broadcasting that refers to a reporter speaking live on air with a presenter in the studio. I had never been on television, except as an extra on AJE's launch day. Now, in the middle of the night, I was being asked to report on a breaking story.

Amal hung up, but not before giving me one last piece of information: 'Sherine, be very careful on your way in. Al Jazeera Arabic sent two people to film the clashes, and now they're in hospital.'

I jumped out of bed with an urgency befitting the moment but with no idea what to do next. *Call someone? Put on make-up? Brush my hair? Pray?!* I realised that I should definitely switch off the Meg Ryan movie.

I suddenly felt like I didn't want this. I had come to Lebanon as a junior producer, to help out in the office with logistics. I wasn't prepared; I didn't have the right clothes, or the right type of foundation for television. I'd done a couple of mocked-up practice interviews when I was in London, but never any real breaking news. I considered calling Amal back and telling her I wasn't well, but I knew what my father would have said if he had been there. I could see his face telling me that this was what I had come here to do.

I quickly got dressed in blue jeans and a dark-green cotton shirt I had bought with Rula, grabbed my make-up case and headed down the corridor to the stairs. I didn't know if the electricity was still on or whether the lift was working, and anyway,

I wasn't ready to face the elevator with all its mirrors and bright lights.

As I approached the lobby, I could hear shouting. The two guys who usually did the night shift behind the reception desk were crouched down by the side of the front doors, yelling across to the manager, who was reading the newspaper and smoking a cigarette as if nothing was happening. As soon as he saw me, though, he got up, dropping his cigarette as he walked fast towards me.

'Don't tell me you're going out there, Miss Sherine!'

I explained I had to get to the office and that I was going to be on television, ending with, 'I have make-up in my bag,' as if that would silence his objection.

'I think the fighting has stopped now — it's been quiet for about fifteen minutes — but it's still dark,' he said, drawing another cigarette from the pack in his pocket.

'Ali!' he called out to one of the reception staff. 'Walk Miss Sherine to the office at the end of the street, next to Haigazian — you know the place.' I looked up at Ali apologetically.

The journey was uneventful, but at the bureau, the news had sent the producers into panic mode. They gathered around me, shouting bits of news in Arabic from our fixers on the ground, most of which I didn't understand. I felt as if I was drowning in words.

Amal was watching me from her glass office on the other side of the room, a mobile phone held to her ear and a pencil in her hand. She yelled at me to come in and handed me the phone. It was Rula, who was manically trying to get dressed before driving to the office. Rula patiently talked me through the story while I tried to focus — instructing me to start with the latest, the clashes, where they were happening, and who was involved. And then the context: the fact that this was coming at a time of heightened tension in the country, and the unrest was spreading beyond Beirut. When she finished, she ordered me to recite back to her exactly what I was going to say. 'Don't look at your notes,' she warned, 'you can't read; you have to be comfortable with the information. Absorb it, or you won't sound credible.'

I ended the call and found multiple text messages from my mother asking if I was all right. I had been on the phone with Rula for less than ten minutes, but that was enough to induce panic that I hadn't replied to her. I messaged her back, explaining that I hadn't forgotten our deal, rather it was the middle of the night and I hadn't wanted to wake them. But I should have known she would be up, watching the news and checking exactly where the violence was in proximity to my hotel. Waking up my father and explaining to him what was happening. She barely slept when I was on assignment.

'Okay, I'm sorry, I promise to reply faster,' I finally texted. 'But I have big news: in ten minutes I'll be live on TV!!'

My phone immediately lit up with exclamation marks, as her anxiety transformed into excitement. If only mine would do the same, I thought. I smiled at how quickly she forgave me, understanding what this moment meant for my career. But mainly I think she was excited at the prospect of being able to see for herself that I was okay.

The enemy of a television live cross is insecurity. The first and last rule is to look and sound confident, no matter what. As my friend and colleague Jacky Rowland used to tell me, 'It doesn't matter what is happening around you; just look at the camera and keep going — the viewers can only see you.' If you don't look straight down the barrel of the camera, you look shifty to the viewer — instantly losing their trust. It seems easy enough, until you are actually facing the huge lens.

How you sound is another issue. I spent my first three months with Al Jazeera English taking voice lessons to lower the tone of my voice after a talent consultant they hired decided mine was too high. 'Lower gives you more gravitas; higher tones, on the other hand, make you sound like you're not a person of substance,' Carla, my voice coach, told me. Of course, what she actually meant was that the more you sound like a man, the more seriously people are likely to take you.

It was hard to feel confident, to forget the two years of rejections at the start of my career and the faces of all those who told me I would never make it. To think of myself as a correspondent and not just an exotic translator with a weird accent.

Seated in the black swivel chair in front of the live camera, I kept reciting my mantra: 'I'm a tree, I AM A TREE.' My father had taught me the metaphor when I was a child: trees keep their core solid despite the wind and rains battling them. The branches will sway, the leaves will fall, but the core stays firm, whatever is happening. 'Remember the tree?' he asked me the first time I complained of being teased at school. Since then, I had found it a comforting thought to focus on. Perhaps because it was a good analogy, or because it made me think of him.

The cameraman gave me a small mic to attach to my shirt, and an earpiece.

'What's wrong with you?' he asked, looking genuinely confused. He did this several times a day, every day. He wasn't used to seeing a reporter looking like they were so nervous that they were about to throw up.

Amal smiled at me kindly. 'You're ready, just enjoy it!' she said, trying to sound calm.

I took a deep breath ... 'FIVE SECONDS,' I heard the gallery producer say sternly in my ear. *Okay, this is really happening, I'm about to speak in front of millions of people*, said the voice in my head ... 'TWO SECONDS' ... *Wow, is that how long three seconds feels like?* I told myself to focus, stay calm. 'OKAY, WE'RE ON,' shouted the director ... *Wait, hold on, do I start speaking? Am I on TV right now?*

I heard the presenter introducing himself and the show, telling the viewers that there was breaking news in Lebanon and to stay tuned for the latest from the scene. The director came back in my ear and told me to 'stand by'; they were coming to me next. My heart was beating so hard I was worried the microphone would pick up the sound.

The presenter asked me a question. It was simple, just like we had rehearsed: 'What's the latest, Sherine?' I started speaking but was barely three words in when I realised I could hear my own voice back through the earpiece, a cruel echo that took me by surprise. I stopped speaking, not knowing what to do about the technical glitch. Amal and Ali looked at me, eyes wide; they didn't know I was hearing myself back, and neither did the thousands of people watching me on their screens. They were just looking at this girl, on a chair, who had said a few words and was now staring silently into the camera.

It may have been three seconds before I started speaking again. In television time, that is an eternity. I fumbled my way through the answer, unable to get my words out because I could still hear my voice echoing back at me loudly through my earpiece. I wasn't making sense. I couldn't hear myself speak.

As I continued to talk unintelligibly, my hands began wandering nervously down the sides of the chair. I suddenly didn't know what to do with these two awkward limbs. One of my hands found its way to the chair's lever, and before I knew it, I'd pressed something and dropped down three inches. Not enough to completely get me out of frame — which would have been merciful — but enough for the viewers to see only my forehead, eyes, and the top of my nose on their screens, while the rest of my face was cut off. Ali threw up his hands in panic — or maybe he had given up. I pumped the lever, trying to make my way back up into the camera frame, all the while continuing to talk about the ramifications of the clashes in this very fragile country. I ended my update then handed back to the presenter.

The director didn't thank me. The presenter didn't ask me a follow-up question. In fact, there was silence all around once I was done. I sat on the chair in the now empty room, breathing deeply to try to calm my racing heart. When I called to ask my mother how she thought it had gone, even she could only muster up a consolatory, 'I'm sure everyone will forget about it; there are a lot of things going on.'

I couldn't imagine a time when I'd be able to go confidently on television. The only good thing was, having started so extraordinarily badly, surely it could only get better.

5.

No Way Out

The American Colony Hotel in East Jerusalem is where seasoned foreign correspondents come to mix with senior diplomats and high-ranking UN officials. The loud whispers, and tongues loosened by alcohol, make it a useful place to find out the news of the day, and what your competitors are doing to cover it.

I was excited to be staying there for a few days, in one of the small rooms just off the courtyard. Al Jazeera's Jerusalem bureau chief at the time, Nick Toksvig, would meet me every morning at the hotel, where an elegant breakfast was served outside, among palm trees, on beautifully tiled square tables. Nick wasn't like other bureau chiefs; he had a soft spot for the newbies. The underdogs who, like him, didn't come from an established pedigree of reporters. He had watched my nightmare television debut and sent me several emails with advice on how to pace myself for my next appearances. His messages always ended with, 'You're a

natural.' It made me feel good, even though I wondered if he said
that to everyone.

By the time I left Lebanon in late May 2008, Hezbollah and
the government had reached an agreement. The deal created
a new national unity government, giving Hezbollah enough
cabinet seats for veto power, which was the group's key demand.
Everyone claimed victory, and Lebanon looked to have averted
another civil war. Or at least postponed it. During that time, I
had managed several more live appearances without clamming
up or falling off my chair, but they were not moments of television magic. At one point, I got so flustered during a live cross
from a very noisy protest that I didn't realise I was on air, missed
the presenter's question, and started fixing my hair in the camera
lens, as if it was a mirror, while thousands of bewildered viewers
watched.

Luckily, my bosses thought my scripted reports, resource-
fulness, and ability to connect with people on the ground made
up for my less-than-polished live shots. I was sent back to
Lebanon and Syria several times, and by November I had done
enough competent crosses to be trusted. When Nick asked my
bosses in Doha to send me to Jerusalem to cover for one of his
correspondents, they thought it would be the perfect opportunity for me to try a different story.

Nick enjoyed it when there were visiting reporters from
Doha because it meant that he could gossip about what was
happening back at headquarters: who was dating who, who was
getting promoted or sacked. But he especially liked mentoring
me, and in turn I enjoyed Nick's company. It was light and joyful;
he was also one of the funniest people I had ever met.

One morning, after helping himself to my pot of tea, he lit a cigarette and leaned back in his chair, looking at me as if trying to work out my mood.

'I know you're not a fan of Gaza,' he began, with his brows lifted, trying to sound boss-like, 'but there's nobody else,' he said, quickening his pace. This was a lot more serious than I was expecting this early in the morning. 'We need you there, I'm afraid,' he finished, saying it so fast I hardly caught the words.

'Anywhere but Gaza, Nick. Please!'

I had gone to Gaza once, right at the start of my assignment, mainly out of curiosity. Just 24 hours was enough for me to decide that I never wanted to return. Gaza had a way of sucking the happiness from you as soon as you arrived, as though it was patrolled by Dementors from *Harry Potter*, ghouls that appear out of nowhere — and before you know it, you can't remember anything good about your life, nor can you imagine anything good ever happening to you again. In Gaza, the Dementors seemed to be everywhere, draining hope and feeding on widespread misery and despair.

The small territory is one of the most densely populated areas in the world. I've often heard it described as an open-air prison, but that's a false analogy. Prisoners are arrested, charged, and tried. In Gaza, your crime is simply being born in Gaza.

The Gaza Strip has been besieged since 2006 by Egypt on one side and Israel on the other. Inside, the Islamist group Hamas controls the ministries and the general running of the territory on behalf of a Palestinian population that increasingly wants nothing to do with them. Together with other armed groups, Hamas regularly fires projectiles into Israel as part of what the group calls their resistance to the occupation. Most of their rockets fall short, at times killing and injuring Palestinians, or else are stopped by Israel's state-of-the-art Iron Dome missile defence system. Nonetheless, for Israelis living in the border towns surrounding Gaza, sirens and shelters have become part of everyday life.

In an effort to contain Hamas, Israel inflicts what can only be described as a policy of collective punishment on Gaza, closing crossing points and controlling everything that goes in and out of the territory, from people to food to plastic cups. One summer, without warning, Israel decided to ban coriander, chocolate, and children's toys.

Gaza is tiny, 40 kilometres long and barely 12 kilometres wide. The Israeli army controls the skies above it as well as the water around it — Palestinians are allowed a maximum of three nautical miles from the shore before being stopped (often with gunfire) by a navy vessel. The land border is surrounded by troops, a fence, and a buffer zone that extends several hundred metres into the territory. At the southern end of Gaza, Egypt controls the Rafah land crossing and keeps it closed the majority of the time. There are almost two million Palestinians trying to survive in this stranglehold, and the vast majority of them are under the age of 25, which means they have lived at least half their lives under siege.

Nick continued to discuss the deployment with me, ordering more tea while he tried to lift my spirits. It was 2008, and the global media's attention was elsewhere. 'You are more likely to get airtime in Gaza than Jerusalem. Everyone is focused on US election night — believe me, nothing is going to trump the imminent arrival of America's first Black president — but if anything does happen, you will be in exactly the right place,' he said, sounding just as persuasive as the other dozen Middle East analysts having their breakfast around us.

I wasn't convinced. We already had one correspondent inside Gaza, Ayman Mohyeldin, an Arab American journalist considered by our editors to be the rising star of the channel. He had come from CNN, where he had done stints in Iraq and Palestine. We had met in Doha several times after the launch and become friends, but he was much more experienced than I was. They would never ask me to go on television over him.

'I'll be straight with you: headquarters want a reaction piece from Gaza the morning after the election,' Nick continued. 'You know, what do people there think of Obama, what are Hamas saying — and Ayman will be busy with an interview we've set up with the Hamas prime minister.'

Immediately, I was irritated. I knew this routine well after my Lebanon reporting experience. All the big shots would be tasked with the main coverage. When they needed to rest, the B-list reporters (me) would be expected to step in to fill airtime at ridiculous hours when nobody was watching. I'd work on a piece all day only for it to be dropped when something more newsworthy happened.

Nick seemed to be reading my mind. 'Listen, just go in for a couple of days to cover the gap, have a nice fish meal on me while you're there,' he joked, reaching into his pocket and giving me 20 Israeli shekels, equivalent to six US dollars.

Gaza was not usually a place you went to relax, but it'd been relatively quiet since an Egyptian-brokered ceasefire had come into effect months earlier. As Nick said, if anything did happen, at least I could maybe get in a couple of live crosses for practice.

I thought for a moment before relenting.

'Okay, Nick, just for you. I think I can survive a quick trip to the Gaza Strip.'

———

'Merry Christmas!' the waiter squealed, with a thick Gazan accent and an extra-large smile. The word 'Christmas' seemed to last a few seconds more than it needed to. He placed the hot chocolate I had ordered on the table in front of me and walked off humming some version of what I think was 'Jingle Bell Rock'. As usual, it was just hot milk, not a speck of brown powder in sight. I didn't have the heart to call him back and tell him this wasn't hot chocolate, nor to inform him that Christmas was two days ago.

I looked up and saw Ayman Mohyeldin coming towards me, weaving through the tables and chairs in the cafe, smiling and nodding at the other customers. It looked like every table he passed automatically paused their conversation to stare up at him. At six foot four, it was hard for him not to make an entrance, but Ayman had lived in Gaza so long it was quite possible that all two million residents knew his name.

In Doha, Ayman had taken me under his wing after I'd told him I wanted to be a reporter. He was a *halfie*, too: his parents were from Egypt and Palestine, but he had grown up in the US. He also loved English Premier League football, and we regularly snuck away during quiet shifts to watch matches in the newsroom cafeteria. When he took the Gaza correspondent position, we kept in touch, speaking regularly about work and our personal lives. He encouraged me to think beyond the cosmetics of broadcast news and identify the deeper message we wanted to send. Like Rula, Ayman let me in on all the reporter's secrets, including how to stay sane in the job. His first tip was that I should always unpack as soon as I got home from an assignment, however little time I was back for, so that I felt grounded. It was Ayman who took me to buy new luggage. 'You can always tell the rookies from their luggage — they're the ones still using old bags their mums gave them when they were leaving for college,' he said to me once as we walked through the Victorinox store in Doha. Al Jazeera may have given me the job, but it was friends like Ayman who made me into a reporter. He was one of those people born to tell a story. His older brother later told me that Ayman used to hold a remote control up to his mouth and pretend to be a reporter when he was a child.

'Hot milk? Are you just waking up or about to go to sleep?!' Ayman chuckled, throwing his phone and wallet down on the table next to my mug and copy of John Grisham's *The Innocent Man*. Ayman and I usually met at the office in the mornings, but it was Saturday, and we had decided that after working long hours for the past few weeks, we should take a day off. I had told him all I wanted to do was sit in a cafe and read an easy book, like a normal person.

My one-day deployment to Gaza had turned into almost two months. The day I'd entered, 4 November, the same night as the US election, Israel had conducted a deadly raid into the Gaza Strip and Hamas had retaliated — officially ending the ceasefire that had been brokered by Egypt. I had spent the following weeks with Ayman reporting on a growing humanitarian catastrophe as the siege of Gaza tightened. Any concerns I had had going in about being treated as a fill-in while Ayman covered the main story had quickly dissipated. There was so much work, so many stories, we could barely keep up. Israel was sporadically opening and closing the crossing into Gaza for journalists — sometimes it was closed for days at a time. Meanwhile, talk of a full-blown war was growing as both Hamas and the Israeli army tested each other's limits.

I played around with my hot milk, using a small spoon to fish out a slimy layer of fat that had formed on the surface, while Ayman read the Arabic newspapers. The coffee shop we were in, Mazaj, was the only decent place to sit and have a sandwich. The shop consisted of two wide floors, and Ayman and I always sat on the upper level, which had a large window overlooking the street below. It wasn't a pretty view — even the main street in Gaza City was rotting under scattered garbage and broken pavements — but at least there was good light. Several tables were scattered around the room, their legs propped up with bits of paper to keep them from wobbling. The chairs were all different colours and styles, and there were a few couches in the corners, with large cushions covering the places where the fabric was torn. The paint was chipped, the hardwood floor heavily stained. Despite the fact that it had just opened, Mazaj — like everything else — looked like it was tired of life in Gaza.

I opened my book, ready to engross myself for the next few hours in something other than Israeli–Palestinian politics and the misery of the siege. Sinking into the soft seat, I read the back cover first — it promised to make me angry at the injustice of America's legal system and the use of the death penalty. *That won't happen*, I thought, *I refuse to get angry today*.

I was barely three pages in when I felt a strong gush of air, followed by a loud thud so intense that it went straight through my body and shook my insides. The ground moved, as if a small earthquake had hit. Suddenly, I was acutely aware of how elevated and exposed we were on the upper floor.

People in the cafe stopped talking and looked around, as if waiting for someone else to lead the panic. The waiter rushed up the stairs, breathlessly telling us not to worry because it was *probably* a 'sonic boom', something we had all become accustomed to — Israeli jets flying close to the coast often let out a terrifyingly loud 'boom' sound. Palestinians say the point is just that — to terrify. Otherwise, it's a harmless gust of wind.

But even the cheery waiter didn't seem convinced, and neither were the rest of us, sitting frozen in our chairs like children waiting for instruction. When we heard a second loud bang moments later, we all knew it wasn't just a sonic boom. Ayman grabbed his wallet and keys, left a 20-shekel note on the table, and said decisively, 'Let's go.'

Downstairs, customers had already started gathering at the door of the cafe and on the pavement in front. We pushed past the crowds, unsure of what they were all looking at but determined to get ahead of them. As I crossed the street to our car, my heart beating fast, my breaths quick and shallow, I looked around but saw only people — *maybe it* was *nothing*, I thought. Then, from between two buildings in the distance, I saw a massive circle of black smoke racing up to meet the sky. *Is that the police station on fire? Is that what was hit? Was it a missile?* There wasn't time to decide; Ayman was already starting the car and pressing the accelerator just as I was putting my second foot inside the vehicle. I slammed the door closed before it flew off its hinges.

It was only a short drive from the coffee house to the office. The roads were manic, cars driving on the wrong side, people warning each other not to go down this or that street as we swerved to avoid flying shrapnel. Out of the window I could see residents running from house to house, calling out for missing members of their families. In the few minutes it took to get back, we heard another four explosions close by, the time between each strike getting shorter and shorter. Now there was smoke everywhere, spreading in all directions so that we could no longer see clearly beyond a few feet in front of us.

Ayman was on the phone to the executive producer in Doha, who had put him on speaker so that everyone in the newsroom could hear him describe the scene. We stopped the car outside the office and made our way up the stairs to the live position on the roof of our building, as producers in Doha shouted down the phone to us, relaying information coming in from the news agency Reuters.

'We need a cameraman, or at least a camera!' Ayman shouted at me. In a twist of fate, our entire Gaza staff — including the cameraman and producer — was in Doha doing the mandatory training for journalists working in conflict zones, called Hostile Environment and Emergency First Aid. We had nobody to operate the camera or live position, or to do the coordination.

'Go and see who is available next door and can help us out; I'll stay on the phone with Doha,' Ayman said, one ear to the phone and the other covered by his hand so that he could hear over the sounds of the explosions and sirens.

By 'next door' he meant the Al Jazeera Arabic office down-stairs. They had been generous in sharing their staff with Ayman and me while ours were away. My body moved mechanically, my legs trying to keep up with the pace of my brain. I tried to focus on the task and ignore the enormity of what was happening.

But there was something distracting me, something I had been dreading from the moment I heard that thud. I had to call my mother. I took out my phone and dialled her London number. I was praying she wouldn't pick up, bargaining with God to give me more time. The next five minutes of my life were not going to be easy.

'Hello.'

'Oh, hi, Ma — how are you? Sorry to call you early.'

'Sherine, what's wrong?'

She was on to me.

'Nothing ... well, no, something ... Mum, Israel is bombing Gaza quite hard, but it should be over soon [a lie] and I wanted to call so you know everything will be okay and that the reporters on TV calling it the start of a war are just exaggerating [another lie].'

My mother started crying; she could hardly speak through the breathless, loud sobs. I thought of her sitting there next to my father, covered in tears, both of them surrounded by pictures of Jesus. Ever since I'd entered Gaza, she'd been afraid of exactly this moment. There was no compromising this time, no attempt to mask her fear with words of support or just staying quiet. She just kept telling me to get out of there.

I tried to reassure her, but eventually I lost my patience. 'It's my work and it's my life,' I shouted, enraged. Again, I was being made to feel guilty about pursuing my own path. Why couldn't they just support me right now? She stopped speaking, and for a few seconds I could only hear quiet sobs. The more guilty I felt, the more I shouted at her to stop crying. I couldn't stop myself, even though I knew she was right to be scared. What a burden it was for her to love me so much. She and my father had spent their lives building protective walls around me, and now I had smashed them down. Worse, I had taken advantage of all their support and encouragement and walked straight into the most dangerous situation imaginable.

At one point, my brother, Raf, grabbed the phone. He was living at my parents' house with his new wife while they searched for their own place. I imagined him waking up to the sound of my mother's cries and running into my parents' bedroom — understanding when he saw her that it was me, again, causing all this pain. He began by telling me calmly how afraid they all were: 'You don't understand, you think your life is just *your* life — but if something happens to you, it's my life, too, that's ruined, and Rania's and our parents'. It's not just *your* life, Sherine.'

Growing up, the only time my brother ever got upset with me was when I let in an easy goal playing football in the park. Even then, he made excuses for me in front of his friends — slippery grass, sun in my eyes — so that nobody blamed me. He would never let anyone say a word against me. I suspect that's why he always insisted that I play on his team.

I was taken aback by his frankness and emotion; I had never heard him sound so distraught. After a brief silence, I ended the call, saying I had to get back to work. I grabbed an available cameraman from Al Jazeera Arabic and went back upstairs to see Ayman, pushing my mother's pleas and my brother's reproach to the back of my brain where I didn't have to feel them.

By midnight, Israel had declared war on Hamas, calling its military offensive Operation Cast Lead and making it clear the bombardment was only day one of the campaign. Israel's defence minister, Ehud Barak, promised the operation would 'expand as necessary', and Hamas swore they would retaliate.

Israeli bombs killed over 190 Palestinians and wounded 250 more in the first 24 hours of the war. It was one of the bloodiest days in the Israeli–Palestinian conflict for decades. Israel insisted it was only targeting 'Hamas infrastructure'. One of the deadliest strikes hit a police academy ceremony. I watched the footage later that evening — the bodies of newly graduated officers were piled up on the cement floor, surrounded by those of their wives and children, all dressed up in their best clothes. Some were still holding their bloodied diplomas.

By the time I had a moment to take in what was happening, the sun was starting to rise. It was around 7.00 am when Ayman and I collapsed on the couch, relieved to be briefly out of the cold and sitting down. We had stood on the rooftop for more than 15 hours, as explosions went off in all directions and planes whizzed past us in the small patch of sky over Gaza. Apart from the few minutes we had while guests and analysts spoke, or promos played, Ayman was giving continuous live updates about the situation and showing viewers the buildings around us that were on fire. We had informed the Israeli army where we were and given them the coordinates of our building so that they didn't bomb us, but their answer was that as long as we remained in Gaza, they couldn't guarantee our safety.

Indoors felt less exposed. At least there were walls between us and the explosions. We called the news desk to ask what the coverage plan was. If this was going to be a sustained military campaign, we needed backup — a few more correspondents and definitely camera operators, producers, and equipment, including bulletproof vests and helmets. I quickly made a list of what we were going to need.

There is a guilty excitement in newsrooms when these types of events happen. When you are not in the field, you can say things like, 'Hundreds are dead, their homes destroyed,' without imagining a single face or building. That's the luxury of distance. But it's different when it's happening around you. From where Ayman and I were sitting, the thudding sounds of bombs, punctured by screams and sirens, were painfully real and present.

To avoid the excited small talk on the phone to the news desk, Ayman and I launched straight into the resources we needed to keep the coverage going. Seconds later, we were interrupted by one of the news editors.

'Ayman, Sherine ... the Erez crossing into Gaza is closed, and Israel has no intention of opening it to journalists, aid agencies, or anyone else,' he explained, patiently but also sounding surprised we weren't already aware of this.

'We can try getting stuff in through the smuggling tunnels along the Egyptian border ... but, no, it's too risky, because Israel is bombing them, too.'

The line went silent as we absorbed the news, and then Nick joined the call from Jerusalem: 'Guys, you know that the other networks pulled their people out before Christmas, right?' We had been so busy the last few days, I hadn't noticed that *everyone* had gone.

'Okay, so?' I asked, confused about why this was relevant.

'So?! So, you and Ayman are the only foreign correspondents inside the Gaza Strip! You are the only ones covering this war from the inside for the English-speaking world. It's unbelievable!' Nick said.

I looked at Ayman, his eyes growing wider as the enormity of the news set in. He had been in war zones before. He knew what these moments meant to big networks — and this time, there would be no competition. But I could only think about one thing: if nobody was coming in, then nobody — including Ayman and me — could leave. We were trapped inside Gaza, just like everyone else.

Strangely, the thought brought on a sudden rush of relief. I felt my muscles unclench as I realised that there were no longer any choices to make about whether to stay or go. I wasn't a bad daughter anymore. I couldn't do as my mother asked and leave, because there was no way out.

'Don't worry,' Ayman said, trying to read my face. Ayman had become a protector, mentor, and confidant during the past few weeks of our reporting in Gaza. He had carefully coached me, pushing me to the outer limits of my comfort zone, showing me how to turn mountains of information and analysis into bite-sized portions of news. We had become a good team. In me, Ayman saw the humanity and empathy he sometimes needed more of in his own reporting. In him, I saw the raw talent and effortless confidence I lacked in mine.

I looked at Ayman, phone still in hand, trying to smile.

'It's just you and I, Sherry,' he said. 'And the war around us.'

6.

House of Healing

During the bombardment it felt as though there were no sunrises or sunsets, no meals, none of the usual markers indicating the end of one day or the start of the next. Instead, we fell into a brutal routine of waking up, going to the roof, calling our contacts, visiting the hospitals, returning to the roof — and so on. I normally used exercise to control my stress levels, but with no gym in sight I sprinted up and down the stairs in our building whenever I could, just to feel that familiar rush of endorphins. My only real comfort was that I was with Ayman, whom I trusted to make decisions for us.

I didn't want to be on television because I was convinced the audience would see through me and realise I was terrified. Instead, I carefully collected facts and figures for Ayman to use in his updates. Finding out how many rockets and mortars were being fired at Israel was the easy part. The Israeli army had set up a number anyone could call, manned 24/7, to give the media a steady flow of information. They were efficient and clear — a well-oiled machine telling us in real time with the appearance of neutral, professional accuracy about the attacks against Israel. There was no way to verify the information, so the best we could do was attribute it to the Israeli military.

On the other side, confirming anything about what was happening inside Gaza was significantly harder — there was no Hamas hotline. In fact, you could barely get hold of any officials inside the Strip because they were mostly hiding underground. Information about casualties had to be collected by calling doctors, and sometimes visiting hospitals and counting the dead and injured ourselves. In our makeshift Al Jazeera newsroom in Gaza City, my colleagues from the Arabic channel and I kept a casualty count on the whiteboard — every evening we logged the total on the side and started again. We tried to note every person's name and age, but as the numbers rose into the thousands that became impossible. The board wasn't big enough.

We spent much of the day in the city's hospitals, reporting on how ill-equipped the facilities were to deal with the overwhelming number of casualties. Ayman relentlessly reported from inside hospital units, challenging Israel's narrative that Hamas was the only target by exposing the disproportionate number of women and children being injured and killed in the strikes. It was clear to us in the first days of the war that the aim was not just to destroy Hamas infrastructure and the weapons being used to attack Israel. It was a war designed to bring the Palestinian population to its knees.

Ayman was meticulous in the language he used to explain

both Israel's aggression and Hamas's firing of projectiles. For decades, Israel has successfully influenced much of the terminology the English-language media uses to describe the conflict, dominating the narrative and trying to advance the idea that their occupation of the Palestinians is both necessary and legal. They call their military the Israel Defense Forces, or IDF, to suggest that its existence is solely about self-defence, and describe their regular strikes on Gaza as 'responses' to particular incidents, as though they never instigate them. Israeli officials brand anyone who resists the military a 'terrorist', and those who question Israel's methods are often labelled 'terrorist sympathisers' or even accused of being anti-Semitic.

The Israeli government's statements and press releases consistently present the conflict as if it were a battle between two equal sides, and it is very effective at getting others to adopt this message, despite the fact that Israel's military, weaponry, and training far outweigh those of Palestinian armed groups. The propaganda has become so widely accepted that reporters covering the story fear looking biased by saying the simple truth — that the conflict is skewed, and one side has a huge amount more power and resources than the other.

This was the context in which Ayman did his reporting, and it wasn't easy. It required staying vigilant and thinking hard before repeating any statements. He was questioned about why he was highlighting the ongoing siege of Gaza and the wider Palestinian occupation in his reports, as if that showed bias, when in fact he was explaining the root cause of the conflict, which was always relevant. To omit it would have been mystifying. But being Arab, and of Palestinian origin, he knew better than anyone that he could not afford a mistake in his reporting, so he refused to rely on any information he couldn't check himself, resisting pressure to report a big attack until he knew all the details and had made his own calls to verify what had happened.

Despite Ayman's efforts, it felt as though the official Israeli narrative — that Gaza was a territory full of little else but terrorists out to destroy them — was succeeding in dehumanising Palestinians in the eyes of the world. Even when our reports showed men, women, and children locked in a confined space and being killed in their thousands, not only was there a lack of outrage, there were no real calls for accountability. President-elect Barack Obama stayed silent, insisting that only President Bush could speak for American foreign policy and that his team was monitoring the situation.

On the evening of the fourth day of the war, as we were walking back to our car outside the main hospital in Gaza City, I noticed a guy selling sandwiches from a food cart. He had a small torch shining down on a metal fryer, where little round falafel sat sizzling in bright-yellow oil. I felt my lips moisten with the prospect of finally getting some hot food. We had been eating tinned meat and tuna for days. But as I approached the cart, Ayman stopped me, grabbing my arm and pulling me back towards him. 'It's getting late; we should head back to the office — the guys will have something for us to eat there,' he insisted. I reluctantly agreed, less because I was worried about being late and more because I knew those greasy sandwiches weren't good for me.

Fifteen minutes later, as we drove back to the office, we heard another loud explosion. The radio announced a hit to the car park of the hospital, where the food cart had been. Ayman looked back at me. 'I think I just saved your life,' he said.

'You,' I said, the shock prompting a moment of dark humour, 'and my effort to eat less fried food.'

It was widely believed by Israeli intelligence, and even some Palestinians, that below the main hospital was a network of tunnels where the Hamas leadership and their military wing were bunkered — essentially using the hundreds of injured civilians in the hospital above as human shields. This presumption was never proven, yet Israel used it to justify attacks near — although never directly on — the hospital, like the one that blew up the food cart.

The hospital itself, called the Shifa (or *Dar Al Shifa*, meaning 'House of Healing'), was a giant complex composed of various medical units and rooms. Until 1948 it had been the only hospital in Gaza, and before that, when Gaza was under British mandate, it had been a British army barracks. It became a focal point for reporting during the war, a place where local journalists could not only log casualties, but speak to people coming from all over the Strip about what was happening in their neighbourhoods.

During the war, it was normal to hear screaming at the Shifa. A lack of adequate medical equipment and drugs, including anaesthetic, meant that even major procedures were done without drugs to numb the pain.

One time, I had separated from Ayman to gather information about the casualties in another unit, and I heard a different kind of scream. Not loud and full, like screams of pain, but short and breathless. I couldn't make out the words, but they were desperate. Someone was calling for help. I followed the noise and found myself at the foot of another familiar building. This one I had been avoiding: it housed the fridge where they put people after they died. Early on in the war, I had spent the day outside it, speaking to people looking for loved ones. They would go inside, where a man opened up the little metal doors with the bodies behind them so that they could see if they recognised their relatives. I hated that room.

I found the woman who was screaming kneeling down on the ground, her hands slapping her face so hard her cheeks were bright red. She gazed up at me, but instead of looking distraught, she smiled. 'He's still alive,' she said, gesturing to the door.

'What are you talking about?' I asked her in Arabic. She motioned at me to go inside. 'You won't believe it. Go and see,' she said, shaking her head. I reluctantly stepped inside the room. There were dozens of separate compartments along the wall, each with space for one dead body. I had heard from people I interviewed that sometimes they put more than one body into each compartment because they had run out of space.

As I entered, I could see two men frantically trying to open one of the compartments at the back, using their hands and feet to pull against a lever that appeared to be jammed. 'Go and get someone to help, we don't have time, go!' one of the men said to the other.

Then I heard it. A banging noise was coming from the fridge compartment. A man was shouting with his last breath, using all his might to push against the door. He was screaming, 'I'm still alive.'

Such was the inconceivable chaos of this war. Injured people with limbs blown off who should have been on operating tables were instead lying on the pavements outside overflowing clinics. Dismembered body parts could be found on the floors of hospitals, among screaming people. There was not enough gauze, not enough medical staff, not enough medicine. And now, even the dead were rising.

Years of Israel's blockade of Gaza, and the most recent restrictions imposed since the end of the ceasefire, had taken their toll, and now everything was running out. The toughest part was watching the innocent suffer. Men, women, and children were being denied their basic right to flee or to access life-saving medical care.

As I tried to find Ayman to tell him about the chaos at the fridges, I noticed an injured boy by the hospital entrance. His slight body was lying flat, pressed against the dark-blue floor tiles. He was maybe 12 years old. I remember noticing the beginnings of a little moustache above his lips. His limbs were long and delicate, his hair black and straight; it looked like it had been drenched in gel. I imagined he was just getting to that age when he would be concerned with his appearance; maybe there was someone next door he had been trying to impress that day, or maybe he had been going out to play football with his friends on the beach.

He was wearing a light-blue shirt that was quickly soaking up the blood seeping from an open wound near his stomach, and was moaning from the pain and hardly moving when I found him. His mother was on her knees next to him. 'They hit our house. We are not Hamas; we are not political. He's just a child, my Ali,' she shouted at me, as if I could have some explanation, some piece of information that would explain this senseless act. The woman was wearing jeans and a dark-coloured shirt, also stained with blood. She looked a little older than me, maybe in her early

30s, the veins in her neck pulsing as she sobbed and looked up, perhaps asking for God's help, perhaps cursing Him for this pain.

We were in a hospital, but there were no available doctors — every one of them had their hands pressing against a wound, stopping blood; pressing hard against a chest, trying to get a pulse; holding a scalpel above a body. There was nobody free, nobody to save Ali. Finally, a doctor walked past us. Ali's mother reached out, grabbing his leg, begging him to help her son, who had now been lying on the floor of the hospital for almost 15 minutes unattended. The doctor turned to face Ali's mother. 'I can't help you, I have to get to surgery,' he replied, looking down at the small child now covered in his own blood, feeling his neck for a pulse. 'This boy is almost gone — may Allah have mercy on him.'

I took off my shirt and wrapped it around Ali's torso where most of the blood appeared to be coming from. But, of course, it didn't help. To stop massive, catastrophic bleeding like that, I would have needed a tourniquet — I knew that from the first-aid training I had been given before my first Lebanon deployment. It was meant to have prepared me for moments like this. But somehow, all that knowledge evaporates just when you really need it. I could feel myself getting angrier as the seconds passed, and I desperately tried to remember something that could help him.

Ali died on the floor in unbearable agony. His mother's face stayed buried in her dead son's chest until they eventually took him away.

I went back to the office and lay down on the mattress, thinking about Ali. Another child killed while the rest of the world went on with their day, another crime committed for which there would be no repercussions. I thought, too, about my family, how worried they were about me, and how I had justified putting them through this by telling myself I was making a difference. But I wasn't so sure that I was.

I was consumed with the idea that I was completely unqualified to report on a war. I kept thinking, if there had to be just one foreign reporter on the ground in Gaza, why wasn't it one of the seasoned correspondents who knew what to do? Like Lyse Doucet from the BBC, whom I had watched on television reporting so eloquently and calmly at times like this, or the famous Christiane Amanpour. Maybe they could have told the story so well that decision-makers would have been forced to stop this madness. I was 27 years old; this was my first big story. It was up to me to convince people to care, I thought, and yet I didn't know how.

Ayman walked into the room and sat beside me. He wasn't the type of friend that hugged; his was a practical kind of love. He spoke gently:

'We have to start humanising the story and showing everyone watching that ordinary people — children — are being caught up in this war.' We had had this conversation already, I thought; when, on the first day of the war, he had tried to convince me to leave Gaza City and start reporting from other parts of the territory, rather than following him around the hospitals all day counting casualties.

I wondered what my mentors would do. Rula and I had talked a lot in Beirut about journalism and the toll it took on our families and lives. I had asked her once if it was worth it, and she had grabbed me with her strong, skinny hands and said yes without hesitation. 'Maybe nobody will ever be put on trial or go to prison for what you see. But once you film it, once you document it, nobody can ever say it didn't happen. That is a kind of justice, too,' Rula had told me.

It was clear that if I was going to stay — and I had no other option — it was time I split up from Ayman so that I could travel around Gaza and show the world what was really going on.

———

When my sister texted me to say our mother hadn't brushed her hair or left the house since the start of the assault a week ago, I knew that she was losing faith I would make it out alive.

My mother was never unkempt, never messy. Even if she was just going to get milk from the shop next door, she was always well put together. Her coat matched her skirt, which matched her bag, belt, boots ... There were never creases in her clothes, which smelled of dry-cleaning. She always wore a gold crucifix necklace, a diamond ring my father had given her when he proposed, and the thick gold wedding band it rested on. She wore make-up and used a wide-toothed comb (never a brush) on her long, brown, salon-washed hair. My friends called her elegant. I asked her about it once, but she laughed and told me that dressing well made her feel good, that it was for her benefit, never for others. Even if you were staying home alone all day, you should be neat and clean, she told me.

She insisted on taking a long bath every morning, into which she poured a drop of dark-green liquid from a small glass bottle labelled Badedas, which she bought in France. On hitting the hot water, the potion exploded, filling every corner of the huge bathroom with mini, cloud-like bubbles that smelled of chestnuts. My grandmother had the same bottle sitting by her bathtub in Cairo. When I was younger, I thought giving up showers and beginning to bathe was a rite of passage for the women in my mother's family. They made it look effortless and normal — as if this was how all adults got ready.

On the first day of the war, after I refused to leave Gaza, my mother bought a second television set. One news channel alone couldn't be trusted to tell the whole story; she needed to know *everything* that was going on in the territory. She placed it next to the main one in the bedroom, near the maps of the Gaza Strip printed on A3 sheets of paper surrounding her bed. The larger of the two television sets showed Al Jazeera English, which she never turned off, not even to sleep. With the information she was getting about the location of the strikes, together with Ayman's updates on Al Jazeera English and her maps, she could trace where I was and which military operation was taking place in that area. That way, she could try to figure out if I was still alive.

By her side she kept her mobile phone, open to a message page that read 'Sherine Gaza Phone' at the top. I barely had time to write and the reception was patchy, so we found a routine: every few hours she messaged 'OK?', and I responded simply 'Y' as soon as I could to let her know I was fine. These letters formed pages and pages of communication that became my mother's lifeline to me.

By her other side, on the floor next to the bed, was my childhood friend Yosra. Her Egyptian parents had been good friends with mine even before we were born; Yosra and I had attended the same primary and secondary schools, and even our universities had been within walking distance of each other. Yosra had spent so much time at my house growing up that she referred to my mother as her 'other mummy'.

She was the only person, apart from my siblings and father, that my mother allowed into the room which my father jokingly called the 'command centre'. Around the same time I joined Al Jazeera in Doha, Yosra had moved from London to New York to pursue her dream of becoming a photographer. When she heard that the war had started, the first thing she did was call my mother. When she didn't answer, Yosra got on a plane to London to be with her.

Every morning, Yosra came to the house and headed straight for the kitchen. Nobody questioned her or asked if she needed anything: Yosra wasn't a guest; she knew where we kept the mugs, the Earl Grey teabags, the biscotti my mother ate every morning. She made my mother and herself milky tea with lots of sugar and sat by her watching the televisions. They hardly exchanged words. 'It's going to be fine, our Shusha is a smart one,' Yosra said, calling me by the pet name she had made up when we were toddlers. But even Yosra's warm energy wasn't making a difference.

The only time my mother smiled was when she saw me appear on television. At that moment, she would shout for my father, who came running up the stairs, and they all watched in silence. I don't think she was listening to what I was saying, nor registering the updates I was giving on the situation. Those she could get from the other channels, from other people's children. She was watching me, my face, the way I moved my body, hearing my voice without listening to the words. On the occasions when my father wasn't fast enough getting up the stairs and missed my update, he asked her what I had said and she replied that she didn't know, but that I had looked tired or sad. Later, my sister told me that my mother's focus was so intense it was as if she was looking through the television, like someone whose whole world was inside it.

———

The first story I filmed during the war in Gaza was about a single mother of four, called Rima Abid.

Rima looked too young and small to have so many children. I think she may have been divorced, but she never mentioned it, so neither did I. In Gaza, it wasn't easy to bring these subjects up, even if you were close to the person. All I know is that her husband was not around, and whatever love the children may have missed out on from their father, Rima was determined to make up for. When she wasn't working, she was with them: playing, cooking, reading stories. They were four beautifully energetic children, one girl and three boys, all under the age of seven. She was the type of mother you felt was growing up with her kids, genuinely enjoying the games and doing their homework with them.

At first, Rima seemed shy and subdued. But when she spoke, she looked me straight in the eyes without fear or hesitation, finding her words easily. If she had been born elsewhere, I imagine she may have been more outgoing. Her quiet strength and intelligence may even have been assets. But under Hamas's conservative rule in Gaza, where women did not enjoy the relative freedom men did, and her single-mother status was a taboo, Rima tried not be noticed.

She lived well, which in Gaza meant she lived in an apartment rather than in one of the refugee camps. From the very first moment I met her, she was warm and generous to me.

It wasn't immediately clear what drew me so strongly to Rima or why I singled her out for that first report, especially since she did not have a dramatic story to tell, like so many others I had met. She hadn't witnessed any massacres or got caught up in an airstrike. She and her kids hadn't been injured or forced to leave their home. When the cameraman suggested Rima to me — she was a distant relative of his — I wasn't sure if she would make a strong enough story.

What struck me, though, was how disarmingly natural she was, seemingly unaware of the camera rolling. Her English was imperfect yet powerful, and a few minutes into the interview she had completely captivated me. As she spoke, I started to realise what drew me to her. Rima felt familiar. She talked about her children like they were everything, with a smile that made her whole face light up. When she told me stories about them, she forgot about the war.

I imagined my mum's look when she saw me on television was the same as Rima's when she watched her children play in the house, as she stroked their hair and smiled at them, softly reassuring them that they were safe.

'I want people in the world to know what's happening to us and to try to put themselves in my place,' she told me. 'All I am trying to do is keep my children safe; nothing else matters. I am not political. I have nothing to do with the resistance. What did we do to deserve this? Nothing,' she repeated, with one arm around her youngest child, squeezing him into the side of her body while the others sat at her feet, cross-legged and listening intently.

As she talked about the first day of the bombardment — racing to the school, which was located next to a police station, for every second of that journey not knowing whether her kids were alive or dead — I was taken aback by the uncontrollable tears rolling down my cheeks. I thought of how my mother, too, must have been feeling on that day and every day since, and I felt her pain acutely. I may have been the one asking the questions, but I was just as vulnerable as Rima and her family. The microphone and bulletproof vest no longer felt like they separated me from any-one else in Gaza. To pretend otherwise was just a delusion.

In Gaza, there was nowhere safe to go, no borders to cross. There were no refugees and no refuge. Throughout the three weeks of the war, as some of the world's most sophisticated weap-onry was used to bomb Gaza from the air, land, and sea, Israel and Egypt kept their borders shut and deprived innocent people of their basic right to seek safety.

I wondered where else in the world that would be allowed to happen.

Rima's children had become terrified of the sounds of war. They could hear the explosions all day, as well as the screams of people on the street and in the nearby buildings that had been hit by airstrikes. They understood what the sounds meant and what they should do. The gush of wind before a strike gave them only a few seconds to hit the floor. The noise of a drone getting louder gave them a little longer to get to their bedroom and hide under the bed. One of the children showed me drawings she had made of F-16 fighter jets, of soldiers walking below them, and of her mother standing by their house with a sign saying '*Salam*' — 'Peace'. 'Mama is there for protection,' she told me. As I spoke to the kids, I thought of the damage this must be doing to their mental health, and whether they would ever recover.

Six-year-old Aseel seemed to be the most affected of the siblings. Rima told me he hadn't left her side for a moment since the start of the war — he even followed her into the bathroom. I told the cameraman to keep rolling and focus in on Aseel. He had big, round brown eyes and dark eyelashes that clung together from all the crying. He kept using his sleeve to wipe his face and nose, before quickly putting his hand back on his mother's skirt.

I asked him why he was so afraid to leave his mother's side, propping up the microphone near his mouth, prepared for the perfect sound bite about how he was scared of the bombs. But Aseel didn't say that.

He stared, emotionless, and replied, 'So that when my mother dies, I die too.'

I lowered the microphone and looked at his little face. Aseel wasn't afraid of being killed. He was afraid of being left alone, alive.

Rima looked at me and nodded; she had heard him say this to her before. She could not allay his fears given that he had understood just how dangerous the reality was. Still, she tried to console and distract the children as much as she could. Every time the bombardment got louder, Rima gathered them on the floor of her living room, away from the windows, and they sang together to mask the sounds of the strikes.

We filmed as they excitedly repeated the same verse over and over. I recognised it as the 'I Love You' song from the children's television series *Barney & Friends*, which was popular when I was growing up.

As I watched them, it suddenly felt like I was back in London and nine years old again — singing church songs with my mother inside our house while the racist neighbour shouted at my father outside.

Just like my mother, Rima was trying to drown out the scary noises for her children. To distract them, for as long as she could, from the reality around them. To make them feel safe, even if they weren't.

I hoped every parent who watched that — whether Israeli, Palestinian, or otherwise — could feel for Rima.

I knew my mother would.

7.

Confessions

By the time Israel announced a ceasefire on 18 January 2009, 1,400 Palestinians had been killed — most of them civilians. Gaza was destroyed. Slabs of cement and craters had replaced apartment blocks and government ministries. In some areas, entire neighbourhoods had been flattened as Israeli army tanks bulldozed their way from the border fence right up to the outskirts of Gaza City. Weeks after the end of the war, rescuers were still finding the bodies of residents underneath the rubble.

The land invasion was the final phase of the assault. But throughout the 22 days, Israeli forces continued their missile strikes from the air and sea. They still said their targets were Hamas fighters and their infrastructure. Senior commanders and factories used to make weapons were taken out. But the devastating number of dead women, children, and elderly Palestinians showed a callous disregard for human life. Meanwhile, Palestinian armed groups claimed victory because they had succeeded in killing three Israeli civilians and a soldier. If they could, they would have killed many more.

The rockets and missiles stopped for a while, but this was not a declaration of peace. It felt more like both sides were exhausted and needed time to regroup. Relations between Hamas and Israel were tense, and the siege around Gaza continued. Rather than marking a new phase in the conflict, the situation deteriorated further for Palestinians.

I left Gaza a week after the ceasefire was declared. What should have been an overnight deployment had turned into 79 days on the ground. The entire staff of Al Jazeera Arabic drove me to the border to say goodbye that morning. Our driver, Rami, who had risked his life every day to take me wherever I asked without question, teared up as I made the long, dusty walk from the Hamas checkpoint to the Israeli-controlled side of the barrier.

I cried, too. Out of sadness, but also because my nightmare was ending. I was finally free to go beyond the remorseless wire fence that had confined me inside a slim strip of horror for months.

I didn't look back at Rami or the others. Instead, I looked upwards, watching the hemmed-in blue space above me expand with every step. My pace quickening in the knowledge that beyond the crossing, into Israel, the sky would be endless.

In a couple of hours, I thought to myself, *I'll be back at the American Colony Hotel.* No doubt, Nick would have reserved a suite for me, one of the nicer ones that overlooked the garden where we had breakfast. The manager would send up an extra-large fruit bowl; maybe he'd add figs and that Jerusalem pear he knew I loved. I would sink into the huge bed with its fluffy duvet, the excess pillows would spill on to the floor, and I would sleep soundly.

I would do all of that because I was not Palestinian. My British passport allowed me access to Israel and wherever else I wanted to go. I had survived the war alongside my Gazan colleagues, stuck inside the tiny territory with them. But now it was over, I was free to leave. They were not.

Rami and the rest of the staff would remain trapped in Gaza, surrounded by the dead bodies and destruction that made it impossible to forget the trauma they had endured. To this day, the siege in Gaza continues, and none of them can leave.

In the months following the end of the war, Ayman and I became celebrities in our small and elite journalist circles. We were invited to talk about our coverage of the war all over the world. We went from conferences in Italy to workshops in France and Ivy League colleges in the United States, where we spoke about our experiences in auditoriums packed full of budding journalists. Magazines and newspapers wrote articles about how we had been the only foreign correspondents inside Gaza, and a prominent Israeli journalist famously declared Ayman to be his 'war hero'.

People were enamoured with the trajectory of an Arab girl, who had lived at home with her parents for 26 years, rising to become one of the main faces of Al Jazeera English. The channel showered us with praise and bonuses, and promoted us on every platform. They made a documentary about our time in Gaza, which aired on both Al Jazeera English and Arabic. Ayman used footage he had filmed of us during the war to make another documentary, which he called *The War Around Us*, and submitted it to notable film festivals.

In the middle of 2009, I took my parents and Amal — our Beirut producer, who had become a good friend — with me to Monaco after one of my Gaza reports was nominated for a Golden Nymph Award. It was one of quite a few prestigious prizes that Ayman and I were singled out for. A year that had started in Gaza with death and destruction was somehow ending with glamour and prestige. At first, it felt strange and uncomfortable to receive these accolades while the siege in Gaza continued, compounded by the destruction from the bombardment. But my colleagues and bosses were telling me that I deserved a break, the war was over and my job was done. I felt as though continuing to experience guilt and trauma, or failure to move on instantly from what I had witnessed would reveal me to be a rookie. Someone who didn't belong in the exclusive club of war reporting that I was finally being let into, a club that wasn't for the weak. It became easier to focus on this new and exciting next chapter in my career rather than what I had left behind in Gaza. And the truth was, too, that I was enjoying the attention, especially from other correspondents who had barely noticed me when I first joined the channel. I ended up spending the summer at my parents' apartment in the south of France, drinking chilled rosé wine and reading on the beach. Not thinking about the siege, or Rima and her kids, or my Gazan colleagues. Not thinking about the fact that they were still stuck exactly where I had left them.

Before my holiday was over, I got an email from my boss offering me a correspondent position based in Jerusalem, covering the Palestinian territories. It was a huge step up from my reporter role, but given the attention surrounding the channel's coverage of the war, the offer wasn't a surprise. Gaza had given me plenty of live practice; I had delivered dozens of reports with almost no help, and performed under immense pressure. My on-air blunders from the past were forgotten, and everything was working out; I would finally be where I wanted to be, reporting the news and shaping people's perceptions of what was happening in the Middle East. I had come a long way from falling off that swivel chair in Beirut. Maybe my old English teacher, Mrs McCloud, was right: I could be whatever I wanted.

Accepting the Jerusalem job was also a way to recompense my lingering guilt over walking away from Gaza the moment the war ended. It was an opportunity to keep following the story of the Palestinians, delving deeper into the occupation and its injustices. I moved to Jerusalem and rented a sand-coloured, three-bedroom house in the occupied east of the city, a short walk from the American Colony Hotel.

Surrounded by greenery, my new house was much larger than I needed. But it reminded me of Number 29 and, following my parents' first visit, it quickly became filled with religious paraphernalia and the smell of incense. The neighbourhood was tense because of the proximity of Palestinian residents to the recent Israeli settlers. More than once, I was pelted with stones by Israeli kids on my way to the grocery store because they thought I was Palestinian. My father bought me a treadmill and put it in the study. He claimed to have found it on sale and got it on a whim, but I was a keen runner and I knew he didn't want me jogging around the area on my own. My mother eased her anxiety by visiting me often under the pretext that she was helping me decorate the house, filling the spaces with huge, comfy white leather sofas and making sure my television played all the movie channels I liked to watch. I soon made friends with a tribe of foreign reporters, and they hung out in my living room eating pizza at the weekend. Before long, I had everything I needed again in the comfortable confines of my new home.

The more I reported from the Palestinian territories, the more I felt a growing sense of unease that I couldn't explain. Spending time in Gaza, covering the aftermath of the war, felt useless. Nothing changed. The rubble piled up on the side of the roads. Barely anything was being rebuilt.

One year on from the ceasefire, Israel's siege was still in place, yet it was as if for the rest of the world the story was over. There were other more pressing events happening elsewhere, and even my own editors started turning down my pitches because it was the 'same old story'. I was stuck. This wasn't the impact I had thought I would be making, and I was tired of feeling guilty all the time.

I keenly felt the injustice that had been dealt out to the victims, and yet the pursuit of justice was not my job. During the war, 344 children were killed by Israeli forces and, despite a UN investigation and an internal Israeli army probe, not a single soldier or official — Palestinian or Israeli — was held to account for the crimes committed. I couldn't help wondering why I had put my family and myself through months of hell.

I made sure to visit Rima and the children when I was in Gaza, but even that became awkward over time. I had promised them when we first met during the war that the entire world would watch their story; over a year had passed, and when Rima or Aseel asked me what difference the reporting had made, I had no answer. If I were braver, I would have told them the truth: it had made no difference. Those who had lost their brothers and sisters, businesses and homes in the war continued to recount their worst moments to me, and I filmed it. But in return, I had nothing to give them. In the end, I was just as unaccountable as those who had taken everything from them. I may not have hurt them, but I wasn't making their lives any better. The truth was, their misery had propelled my success.

It was in this period, as I searched for my ebbing sense of purpose, that I began reading about the great American journalist Martha Gellhorn. After her editors refused to send her to the Normandy beaches to report on D-Day, she dressed in a nurse's uniform and went anyway. For her very first deployment, covering the Spanish Civil War in 1938 for *Collier's* magazine, she crossed from France into Spain alone, with a knapsack and fifty dollars tucked in her boot. But she too struggled, becoming despondent upon her return. She saw that her intrepid reporting from makeshift hospitals, her descriptions of boys in pieces and pools of blood on the roads, didn't change the course of the war. She persisted, explaining in a letter to her friend First Lady Eleanor Roosevelt that she could not give up because, as she saw it, 'The only way I can pay back for what fate and society have handed me is to try, in minor totally useless ways, to make an angry sound against injustice.'

That was how I had rationalised my job: an angry sound against injustice. I told myself that my reporting resonated with people; it had been noticed. People wrote to me from all over the world saying that for the first time they felt sympathy for the Palestinians and understood the conflict better. Surely, I was helping to change the conversation.

But it wasn't enough to satisfy the uneasy feeling growing inside me. Increasingly, the stories I was telling from Gaza after the war were being met with a wall of public indifference, and I doubted whether I was making any difference at all anymore. The angry sound was now barely a whimper. The viewers that did still care about what was happening around the world moved on to other stories and events, and so the news agenda followed. Or perhaps it was the other way around.

I found myself becoming irritable at work, and my friends and colleagues suggested I take a break. The word 'burnout' is used in the media industry a lot to describe everything from falling asleep at your desk to manic behaviour. I knew that something was wrong, but it wasn't the big things that would trigger me, like the pressure of deadlines, long work hours, or even being sent on dangerous assignments. Those things I did almost robotically. Instead, it was seemingly trivial stuff that pushed me over the edge. The first time I felt uncontrollable sadness was when I took a taxi to our office in West Jerusalem one morning, only to realise I didn't have enough change to pay the driver. I broke down, right there in the street, weeping so hard I fell down on my hands and knees, my forehead resting on the kerb.

Eventually, a colleague helped take me back home, where I spent the rest of the day in bed, feeling numb and hollowed out. My head was empty, and I had no interest in understanding why; I only wanted to sleep. The next morning, I went back to work as if nothing had happened. Had I been drinking heavily, turning to drugs, or having nightmares of burning buildings, I would have been sent to therapy and diagnosed with post-traumatic stress disorder. But because the symptoms were more mundane, my sporadic inability to function was passed off as tiredness. I was told that I simply needed a holiday.

At the end of 2010, two years after the start of the Gaza War, Ayman and I were nominated for an International Emmy for our coverage of the assault. At the ceremony, journalist friends were still coming up to Ayman and me, congratulating us, but we didn't end up winning the award. It was yet another sign that the world had moved on from Gaza — to militant attacks in Pakistan, earthquakes in Haiti and Chile, and the massive eruption of a volcano in Iceland, which stranded millions of travellers. The war felt like a distant memory, lost in the fickle churn of the news cycle.

I decided to take an extended break over Christmas and went back home to Number 29. For the next few weeks, I barely left the house and mostly slept. I didn't have the energy to play football with Raf, or even to go for a run. I'd lost my appetite, and my limbs began to thin out so much that I fitted into clothes I had worn as a teenager.

'I have an idea,' my mother said to me one morning, bringing in a breakfast tray with fresh orange juice, sweet tea, and toast. I had remarked once in passing to her that I wanted one of those trays with legs that they have at hotels so that I could eat in bed. I sat up and took the cup of tea, waiting for her to continue. *This had better not be another story about a Coptic friend of hers with a son I should meet.*

It was too early in the morning for one of those conversations.

'If you don't want to speak to your father and me, how about speaking to Abuna?' she continued quickly. 'I know you're fine, but we feel that it would be good for you to talk to someone.'

Abuna, literally 'our father', is the Arabic name for a priest. Every Copt has an *abuna*, who — in theory — they confess to regularly. Your *abuna* is your own personal link to God. Mine was Father Angaelos.

It wasn't the worst idea, I thought, relieved I wouldn't have to think of another excuse to avoid a blind date. Both my siblings were married, and my sister already had two kids. I was behind again.

'Great,' my mother said, taking my silence as agreement. 'I called Father Angaelos already, and he'll be here soon. Get dressed!'

The doorbell rang just as I finished eating the toast. My mother showed Father Angaelos into the fancy dining room, usually reserved for special occasions.

I walked into the room and greeted him. As we sat down, my mother closed the door behind her, smiling to herself at the success of her idea.

Father Angaelos was not your ordinary Coptic priest. He was cool. If Marvel Comics ever created a superhero priest, they would model the character on him. He dressed in a traditional long gown with matching headgear, but he drove a black car with private plates and wore custom-made silver cufflinks in the shape of a Coptic cross, much more elaborate than a normal cross. He made an impression wherever he went, and he counted foreign diplomats and members of the British Royal Family among his acquaintances.

I had met with Father Angaelos many times before, but this time I was nervous. I wasn't exactly sure what I was meant to do.

'Bless me, Father, for I have sinned,' I said, closing my eyes. 'It's been ... Actually, I've not done confession before,' I admitted, opening one eye to see his reaction.

Father Angaelos sat back, leaning into the huge chair with wooden armrests and salmon-coloured silk cushions. Despite only being a few years older than me, he had the presence of a senior statesman — except less corrupt, and with God on his side.

He paused to study my face, a smile spreading as if it could easily turn into a laugh. 'I know you haven't confessed before, Sherine. I've been your priest for ten years, since you were 18 years old. Had you confessed before, it would have been to me,' he said, amused. 'Also, we're not Catholic. You don't need to start with, "Bless me, Father, for I have sinned." This isn't *The Godfather.*'

Father Angaelos uncrossed his legs so that he could get closer to me. The long silver crucifix around his neck slipped to the side as he tugged at his collar. Just like other Coptic clergymen, he had a long beard that reached his chest. It must be a nightmare for him going through airport security, I thought. Although I bet his questioners would be surprised by how charming he is.

'What is it that you're feeling bad about, my dear?' asked Father Angaelos. Something in his eyes told me he wanted a real answer.

I wanted to explain how sad I had been in Jerusalem. To tell him that some days it was an overwhelming effort just to get dressed, and I wasn't sure why. How the only thing I knew how to do was to go wherever my bosses told me to go — the West Bank, Israel, Gaza, wherever — and film whatever story I was instructed to film. I wanted to explain to him how it was easier for me not to think or feel anymore, because when I did, all that came of it was guilt. The outside world thought I was a success, but everyone I loved could see that I was coming off the rails.

'I'm not sure what I'm doing all this for. I am not making a difference,' I said, more to myself than to him.

He probably didn't know what I was talking about, but it felt good to say it out loud. I felt a little lighter, as if he had taken a piece of sadness from me. I wanted him to forgive me for the terrible anxiety I had caused my parents over a job I wasn't even sure I wanted to be doing anymore.

As these doubts crowded in, my foot started shaking, my head felt heavy, nausea was setting in, and tears were gathering, the way they always did when I had these thoughts. Father Angaelos waited for me to continue, but I said nothing.

Finally, he broke the silence. 'You know how very proud your parents ... all of us ... are of you, don't you?' he said.

I nodded and smiled. I had heard that before. There were very few Coptic Christians visible in the media. I knew that my success was important for our community. I witnessed it when I was at church with my parents: friends and acquaintances often asked me for advice about getting into journalism. Suddenly, being a reporter had become a real career option for them, the way it had never seemed for me. Meanwhile, their parents took my mother and father aside, saying things like, 'I don't know how you cope.' I suspected they were thankful to me for representing the community but relieved I wasn't their child, in equal measure.

Father Angaelos glanced down at his watch and, suddenly feeling the pressure of the end of the meeting, I spoke without thinking. 'Abuna, if you could hear inside my head, you wouldn't be so proud.' The words fell out of my mouth before I could catch them. Father Angaelos's eyes and mouth sank downwards, as if he was mirroring what was going on inside me.

He didn't reply. Instead, he sat quietly, listening to me describe how the siege was keeping people living in misery in Gaza and how I didn't want to go there anymore, complaining about my editors who had little interest in the story, and admitting that I myself was starting to lose the very patience and empathy that had made my reporting stand out.

When I finished speaking, Abuna gently placed the silver crucifix dangling from his neck on my head and prayed for me, asking God to forgive all my sins and to continue to protect me. He then opened his arms and hugged me tightly. As I buried my head into the soft fabric of his robe, holding back the tears, I realised that I had just had my first confession.

'I have to go, it's getting late,' he said, releasing me and taking his car keys from the coffee table in one swift motion.

Just then, my mother came into the room. 'Sorry to disturb. Sherine, did you see the news?' she said hurriedly, handing me her phone, which was open to the Twitter app.

'A man named Mohamed Bouazizi in Tunisia — I think he sells fruit or vegetables — he just tried to kill himself after a fight with the police,' she said. 'He actually set himself on fire! Do you think you will have to go?'

As I led Father Angaelos out, he reached into his bag and took out a small rectangular box. 'I got you something,' he said, as I took the box and opened it. Inside was a small black leather note-book. 'It's so that you can write down your thoughts. Confession doesn't have to be done out loud,' he said, smiling as he closed the front door behind him.

———

My parents and I watched events in Tunisia unfold on Al Jazeera Arabic. The protests spread throughout the countryside, and demonstrators were demanding that President Ben Ali, who had been in power since 1987, step down. They blamed him for high unemployment rates, corruption, the inflated price of basic food, and for a decline in civil freedoms. Ben Ali visited Bouazizi in hospital, but it did nothing to calm the protests. On 4 January 2011, Bouazizi died, instantly becoming a symbol of state repression and corrupt power.

Despite technically still being on holiday, I could sense the excitement of the network. Emails flew around analysing what was happening. Planning editors sent their crews to embassies to get visas for countries in North Africa and the Middle East. I hadn't seen this much activity since the Gaza War, and I rapidly felt myself getting sucked in.

Both Al Jazeera English and Arabic were broadcasting live from Tunisia every hour as protests reached the capital, and it seemed the president's days were numbered; all other stories had been put on hold as the network threw the full weight of its resources behind the coverage. It soon branded the protests the 'Arab Awakening' — signalling the start of what it saw as a new era of political and social awareness across the region. People were beginning to wake up to the fact that their countries were being led by tyrants, curtailing their rights and syphoning state funds to benefit themselves and their cronies. They were also realising that they no longer had to accept this, that they could collectively do something to change their circumstances.

This was the moment the network had been waiting for since its inception. If its mandate was to empower the voiceless and expose the corrupt, then this revolt was a natural culmination of those efforts.

When I heard they were sending another round of correspondents to Tunisia, I called the head of news, Salah Negm. I explained that although I was still on extended leave, I wanted to be deployed. I felt an overwhelming urge to be on the ground again, to speak to the pro-democracy protestors and get their message out. It was the first time I had asked something of Salah so directly.

'I appreciate the offer,' he said, 'but we need you back in Jerusalem for now.' There was no room for negotiation, and I was disappointed. President Ben Ali had just fled the country, and Ayman had been sent to Bouazizi's home town and managed to speak to some of his relatives. I was missing an important story, one that had the potential to change the Middle East for ever.

I relented, but not before asking for one last thing. 'If the protests spread to Egypt, I would like to be sent,' I said. 'My family are there. Egypt is really important to me.'

'Tunisia is not Egypt — Ben Ali is not Mubarak. I can't see it happening,' he explained, in a tone so confident I instantly felt foolish. Salah was Egyptian, too, and had spent a lot of time there growing up. 'But sure, at the first sign of serious protests in Egypt, I'll send you.'

8.

The Uncle

I stood on the bridge, looking down at all the tiny heads. It was incredible to watch the protests from a distance. I could still hear the chants of Egyptian women and men who just a week ago had been sitting in their living rooms, watching events in Tunisia and wondering if their time would ever come.

In the corner of this unimaginable scene, the massive headquarters of Egypt's ruling National Democratic Party were burning. Demonstrators had set the building on fire days before, then stayed to see it turn black and crumble, while millions of papers covered in state secrets turned to ash and disappeared in the wind. A defiant echo filled the space where quiet obedience used to be — 'The people demand the downfall of the regime,' they shouted in one angry voice.

Up ahead, lines of demonstrators curved around the outside of a giant circle that on less remarkable days served as a roundabout.

Small, brightly coloured tents filled the grassy ground in the centre. Containers of food, medical kits, and bedding were scattered about, defying any notion that the protestors were going home. They weren't real tents or medical kits, of course; there had been no time for that. These were things born of necessity, made by men and women who had found their purpose in this square and in this moment. Here, what was once a cotton sheet met with a wooden branch and became a way to help keep the cold wind out; goggles for keeping chlorine from kids' eyes were now used to resist tear gas.

This was Egypt's Tahrir Square — *tahrir* means 'liberation'. What could be more perfect?

Salah Negm's prediction had been proven wrong. The pro-democracy protests spreading through the Arab world had reached Egypt. The first mass gatherings of demonstrators happened in the capital on 25 January 2011. Three days later, protestors took to the streets again around the country, clashing with security forces. I had called Salah that morning — this time from Jerusalem — and reminded him of his promise. Egyptian authorities were shutting down the internet, and by midnight the army had been deployed to maintain order as hundreds of thousands protested, demanding that President Hosni Mubarak step down. I arrived in Cairo from Jerusalem in the early hours of 29 January with my cameraman, Brad. A nationwide curfew had just gone into effect.

Despite the restrictions, the protestors on the streets had swelled to numbers never seen before in Egypt, occupying landmarks throughout the country. They had awakened not only to their discontent with the authoritarian president, but to the idea that *they* could make him leave. History had told them this was impossible, but after what had happened in Tunisia, it started to feel not just possible, but inevitable.

A day of reckoning had come for a president who had arrogantly assumed his rule would last for ever. His police had already vanished — ordered to hand over security to the military — and Mubarak had been forced to dismiss his cabinet. His whereabouts were unknown, and world leaders were turning on him, questioning his ability to rule. His party headquarters had been reduced to charred ruins. There was a pride among the demonstrators; they felt that they were in control of their country and their future for the first time.

In the course of my reporting, I slept on Tahrir's ground and ate from its rations. I marvelled at how everyone was provided for equally, from small children to the elderly. How nobody seemed to notice the bitter cold, let alone complain about it. The protestors talked about why they wanted the president and his cronies gone, and how they were determined to break the system that had kept them in a cruel, deliberate cycle of poverty.

Sometimes we switched the camera off and I just sat, sipping strong, hot tea and listening. One woman described how she used to stand in a queue every morning for more than two hours to wait for subsidised bread to feed her nine children. 'The bread, that was our lifeline; I had to get it so we didn't starve,' she told me, waving her hands in a gesture of despair. But on many days, after the long wait, the baker had declared there was no more and closed up for the day.

'I could see a stash of dozens of loaves behind the stall; the seller kept them to give the richer families who paid him double and didn't even queue,' she said loudly, no longer afraid or ashamed to recount the story.

The boundaries between myself and the people I was reporting on began to dissolve, even more than when I had been stuck inside Gaza. I wasn't chanting or holding up a banner, yet in Tahrir I too felt like a protestor. I had witnessed the country's inequalities as a child — the beggars with their hands pressed against my car window, the Coptic kids living in a rubbish tip. In Egypt, for too long shocking sights had been normalised, and anyone who questioned them had been silenced. It was what had made me feel like this country could never really be mine. As if I was an outsider for noticing the discrimination and being angry about it.

This eruption in the square, the feeling among people that they deserved to have their basic rights respected and wouldn't leave until that was accomplished, connected me to them and made it my revolution, too. I felt a sense of purpose return as I reported unfiltered stories of life under Mubarak, giving a voice to those rejecting the corruption.

For the first time since Gaza, I didn't feel sad or guilty. I felt powerful.

Two days after I arrived, my boss, Salah, called and told me to lie low for a while. I didn't want to leave the square, but I had to get off the streets for a few hours, and not just because I desperately needed a shower. The hotel rooms where the rest of our crew were staying, at the Nile Hilton, had been raided by security forces. Our equipment was confiscated and six of my colleagues were detained. Days earlier, Al Jazeera's offices had been sealed shut by plain-clothes police, and we had been officially banned from the country. The authorities had decided that it was Al Jazeera that had planned and instigated the protests, refusing to believe that the anger on the streets was genuine and instead spinning it as a media conspiracy to oust the president. Colleagues from *The Washington Post* had been taken in for questioning. My friend Yosra, who was back in New York and watching news reports on television, told me that US networks were reporting how their correspondents in Cairo were being harassed and intimidated by the authorities. I had been stopped twice by the security forces asking for identification and searching me for any sign that I was a journalist. I had escaped both times by telling them I was a student at the American University in Cairo.

The plan was to visit my uncle Ayad, who lived about an hour away in a compound on the outskirts of Cairo, not far from the leafy neighbourhood where my parents had both grown up. His house would be a good place to lie low, I thought: it was far enough from the epicentre of the protests to be relatively safe. And since the day Adam went missing all those years ago, I had been aware that Uncle Ayad was an important man. His connections with the army had grown, and he still worked on military infrastructure projects while continuing to build some of the city's most iconic structures. With my uncle, I could melt into the surroundings and be just an ordinary Egyptian girl. And, importantly, he was the only person I knew who would find it amusing that I was now an enemy of the state, and who would be brave enough to take me in.

When I called to ask if I could come over, it was as if Uncle Ayad had been expecting it. He gave me clear instructions. I was to wait for his driver, Saeed, on the bridge at the foot of the steep ramp overlooking Tahrir at noon. Saeed knew what to do from there.

I got to the bridge a little early to send off a report that Brad and I had filmed the day before at a prison on the outskirts of Cairo called Abu Zaabal. The jail was notorious for torturing its inmates. My past requests to film inside had been denied by the authorities, so when I heard there had been a prison break, we headed straight there. The prison complex was huge; a labyrinth of grey stone built to house 3,000 inmates and their guards. By the time we arrived, it was empty, like the set of a zombie film. The doors of all the buildings had been left wide open, and scattered belongings — clothes, books, and bedding, perhaps once someone's only possessions — lay abandoned on the dirty roads. The prisoners there hadn't just left; they had run for their lives.

The report was taking time to send because I was using the patchy internet on my phone. Saeed had been patiently waiting in the car for me for more than half an hour. My uncle had called twice during that time. My mother had also called and texted me. But every time I answered, my phone lost reception. She was going to be angry about my communication, and a conversation starting with, 'How difficult is it to send me a one-word text saying you're okay?' was definitely on the cards.

'FILE SENT,' my phone finally read. I exhaled air I hadn't realised was trapped and dragged the file to the wastebasket, shutting the laptop. I gathered the rest of my things and walked down to the car. As I got in, Saeed got out of the car and came around to my side to close my door for me. I grabbed the large black leather handle and looked up at him — willing him with my eyes to stand back as I scanned the periphery to see if any of the protestors milling around were watching us.

For the first time since the uprising started, it wasn't the fact that I was a reporter that I was afraid of exposing, but my privileged identity as part of the Egyptian elite. I couldn't shake off my family connections as easily as I could hide my press card. Saeed sensed my discomfort and backed off. I wondered if he felt it, too: the sense that we were on the cusp of a new reality that was a complete reversal of everything we had known before — where journalists were tolerated, but class hierarchy was not.

The car smelled of leather and jasmine, a bunch of which hung from the dashboard looking tired, dehydrated. The seats, the steering wheel, the dashboard, even the box of Kleenex tissues, were all black. A small silver cross with Jesus on it was attached to the air vent, and I wondered if Saeed, a Muslim, minded staring at that crucifix all day as he drove.

He noticed me shivering and asked if he should turn up the heat. It suddenly occurred to me that I hadn't felt warm in days. Cairo's winters can be brutal, and I had been chilled to the bone in the square, the only warmth I had felt coming from tea that rapidly cooled in my hands, or emanating from the masses of breathing bodies around me.

The roads from downtown Cairo to my uncle's house were notorious for heavy traffic. But the uprising meant that schools and universities were closed, and public services had come to a halt. The swarms of civil servants whose journeys to work usually overloaded the streets with cars and buses all day were gone. There was hardly a vehicle on the road, and for a city of seventeen million people, that alone was remarkable.

As we approached my uncle's neighbourhood, I started to relax — my report was sent, I was warm and safe. I could finally have a shower, wash my hair, maybe even take a nap in a real bed. The house was in a suburban complex that had been purpose-built for a class of Egyptians for whom segregation had become a preferred way of life. These weren't just homes. They were sand-coloured, gold-rimmed mansions with huge pools and endless winding staircases leading up to more bedrooms and bathrooms than their owners would ever need. The complexes had their own infrastructure: separate shops, cinemas, gyms, everything you needed within safe walking distance.

The compound gates looked darker and taller than I remembered. Had the iron bars always been there? The car stopped at the entrance. A doorman I didn't recognise walked towards us, the rim of his long dark gown, or *galabeya*, greyed by the sand his sandals dusted up. He would have looked normal had it not been for the gun he was cradling in his arms.

The expression on his face suggested he was ready for a confrontation. My body tensed, and I held my mobile phone in my hand tightly. In Egypt, people can disappear very fast. I wasn't sure that even my uncle could protect me if the authorities found out who I was.

The complex was on lockdown. 'Who is she?' the man abruptly asked Saeed, as if I wasn't there. 'These people can't just keep inviting whoever they want to come in and out of here as they please.' His tone caught me by surprise. This was usually a formulaic interaction. The doorman was always polite to residents and their guests. Always.

I was startled by what I now recognised to be an anger that went beyond the fight to bring down the president: this was animosity towards the class structure at large. I had felt this instinctively when Saeed had tried to close my door on the bridge, but had pushed the thought away. Wrapped up in Tahrir's ideals of democracy and equality, I had loved the way that the square had brought together Egyptians from across social divides. Among the poor and downtrodden, I had seen people who looked like my uncles and aunts and cousins, with their designer bags and sunglasses, holding signs calling for the president to step down. And the woman who had told me the story of the bread — she was angry at the system, rather than those who had found a way around it. Wasn't she?

Suddenly, the sense of security my privilege had conferred was dissipating. The doorman was still protecting his patrons inside, but for how long? Would people like my uncle lose everything, just like my parents had under the former president Abdel Nasser? They had been uprooted and forced to leave their homes overnight. I kept thinking of my grandfather, pleading with the guard just to let him fetch his glasses so that he could see. I wanted Mubarak and his corrupt regime gone. But I wasn't prepared for a forced demolition of the social order, or a violent turn against those with money. I was afraid for my family. They weren't the bad guys. They had found their way around the system and worked hard for what they had. Surely they didn't deserve to be stripped of their wealth and punished. Surely that wasn't what justice was.

The uprising was for a more equitable system based on liberal values. Not one of forced levelling, but one that gave everyone real freedom and choice. These were not just the utopian dreams of a young reporter; this was the idea the protestors presented, at least those I had spoken with from across the social classes. This was how I reconciled my class with my conscience. I believed in this vision because I needed to. The alternative was to face an impossible choice: family or revolution.

'My uncle, Engineer Ayad, lives here, and I am his niece; he's waiting for me,' I told the doorman, with just enough irritation to sound like I belonged. I was wearing light denim jeans that were stained from days of sleeping rough. My shirt had a rip just under the pocket near my chest, which I had got while jumping over a barbed wire fence to get to one of the protests. Luckily, I had an undershirt on, but that didn't stop the man from staring. 'I'll call my uncle, and you can speak to him on the phone.' I stared back at him, trying to redirect his eyes upwards.

Eventually, he let us drive past. Out of the window, I saw large planks of wood pressed against doors and windows. People had fortified their homes as though we were in a war zone. Men walked around toting small guns and bats, walkie-talkies in their hands like pumped-up militiamen heading to the front line. Aiming to protect families and properties from looters, these armed neighbourhood watch groups had become a common sight around the city, especially in the suburbs. With the police out of the picture, many people were scared for their lives as well as for their possessions, especially in the more remote compounds like the one where my uncle lived.

Residents here had consciously segregated themselves from the poverty and deprivation that existed beyond their walls. In these enclaves, they had found a way to flourish. The uprising was threatening to take down this order because the guarantor of this way of life — the president himself — would be gone. The elite class was not immune from Mubarak's rule of fear or the police's brutality, but they had the means to protect themselves through favours and bribes.

It took a few minutes for the maid to undo the barricade of wooden panels attached to the large double doors of my uncle's house. The house was as exquisite as I remembered, and I was happy to be somewhere familiar, surrounded by an abundance of chandelier-lit furniture and books. The white marble floor where I had played with my cousins as a child was the same. We had slid around in our socks, barely missing the antiques scattered around the house and all the while being shouted at by my aunt.

I followed the maid towards the drawing room, tucking my shirt into my jeans and combing my hair with dirty fingers. Just then, I heard a deep, playful voice emanating from the landing above. 'What have you done to yourself?' My uncle appeared, still wearing his nightrobe, holding on to the banister with one hand as he made his way down. 'You need a shower, my dear. And then we will lunch.' He added, 'I know you love sushi, but your aunt didn't have time to roll any, so we made you something hot instead.'

After lunch, my phone rang. It was the news editor, Rob, congratulating me on the story I had filed earlier. I felt pleased with myself: I knew it was a great story. These were the moments when journalism felt like the best job in the world. I excused myself and went upstairs, taking two steps at a time until I reached one of the bedrooms. It was a small miracle that my phone was even working and the call from Doha had come through. Communication wasn't easy because the phone networks were overwhelmed and the internet still wasn't working properly, unless you were one of the few who had found a way around the government's restrictions.

I listened to Rob tell me how they were planning to give the piece prominent billing in the evening newscast. I asked him whether my colleagues were still in detention, and he assured me they would all eventually be released.

For the second time that day, I relaxed. I thought about quickly texting Yosra and telling her to watch out for my story on AJE. But instead, I hung up with Rob and just allowed my body to sink slowly into the huge bed. There was a soft brown leather reading chair in the corner, and the door to a giant walk-in wardrobe was slightly open, revealing rows of designer bags and shoes. What a contrast to the places where I had spent the last nights.

I contemplated sleep, relieved that my story was now safely delivered. I had done my bit. But it was getting dark, and the curfew would soon set in. There was too much happening, and with my colleagues still detained, I had to keep feeding the news cycle. It wouldn't be long before Rob called back and asked what I was planning to give them next.

I swapped the Juicy Couture tracksuit I had borrowed from my cousin for my freshly washed jeans and a new cotton shirt. *Okay, let's do this*, I rallied, pulling down on the door handle. My hand slipped, and I stumbled backwards. Confused, I tried to remember if I had locked the door when I came in. I didn't remember doing that, but then again, I had been distracted on the phone. I played with the lock, but it wouldn't budge. I tried the handle again — surely it was just stuck. Twice, three times, four ... nothing was happening. It was locked from the outside.

I banged on the door, first with one fist, then with both, until my uncle's voice made me stop.

'Sherine, *habibti* — "my love" — calm down,' he said through the door. 'Your parents called. Everyone is very worried about you. I'm not going to keep you here against your will, of course, but take a moment to think about the danger you are putting yourself in, while I get your tea.'

I suspected keeping me in the room was my mother's idea. My father had probably told her it was a little dramatic, but she would have convinced him it was the only way to try to stop me; he, too, would have secretly thought it was for the best. For the first time, my parents felt they knew the situation better than I did. This wasn't Lebanon or Gaza, this was Egypt — and they had lived through turbulent change here before. It was why they had left. Except now I had come back.

'Uncle, I have to go to work. This is my job,' I said into the silence. 'Please open the door. This isn't funny!'

But he was gone. I understood the intention was to make me think and keep me out of harm's way. But I was angry, just like when my mother didn't want me to leave home for university, and after the call with Raf in Gaza. After all this time, my family still didn't trust me to make the right decision, I thought. They also didn't understand that taking risks was part of my job, and that this time it was important.

At the back of the room, I saw an oversized window. I hadn't noticed it before because it was covered by elaborate curtains held together in the corner with a thick white rope. I undid the tight knot using my hands and teeth, and hurriedly pulled aside the material to look out; I was so frustrated I briefly considered climbing down the side of the house, but we were too high up. Instead, I stared out of the window at the vast mounds of dirt-speckled sand, noticing where it met the red tarmac in the distance, telling myself to be patient.

At least my story will air; that buys me some time, I thought. I still couldn't believe I had filmed inside Abu Zaabal. I had found a small group of prisoners and guards huddled by one of the abandoned buildings. They knew about what was happening in Tahrir and hated Mubarak, whom they believed to be the cause of their misery in sanctioning their illegal treatment. Even the guards joined in. One of the inmates told me he only had a few months left on his ten-year sentence and so didn't want to leave for fear of being re-sentenced. Others said they simply had nowhere else to go. They all spoke about the torture and mistreatment they had endured inside the stone cells, which they shared with upwards of thirty people. There was a cruelty that the regime reserved just for its inmates — silently maiming them in rooms and chambers not fit for anything that breathed. Inside, they said, you don't exist as a human being. You don't exist at all. They described how the floor heated up in the summer so severely it would burn their skin.

'Sounds like hell,' I said.

'But at least in hell you're already dead,' one of them remarked.

Yet, despite all this, they were still afraid to leave the prison. They knew about the deep network of police, informants, judges, and lawyers that worked in unison against men like them. The idea that they would be free once they left the prison was a fantasy, even if the president fell. How could they be free when Egypt wasn't?

The sound of a bolt unlocking jolted me back to reality. I

jumped off the bed and ran towards the opening door. My uncle looked sheepish.

'Here's the tea. You know your mother, all of us, are scared for you. We don't know what is going to happen,' he offered. 'Mubarak won't go without a fight. Things are about to get much worse.

'How about you stay here a few days, just until things become clearer?' he tried again. 'You can use the phone and the computer in my office to do your work, if you like?'

My irritation dissipated. He too was torn, forced to be the mediator, at once the uncle and the brother. I rose up on my toes to touch his cheek with mine. I didn't need to say anything; he knew I had to go.

Uncle Ayad told me his last request was for me to take care of myself and to keep a low profile for the next few days until things settled.

'*Insha'Allah*,' I replied.

I made a deal with him and my aunt that I would stay one more hour and take some food back with me to Tahrir. They didn't like the idea of me living off the street food that the protestors were handing out.

On the way back downtown, I thought about my family and how differently we were experiencing the same events. For me, the rebellion was about Egyptians rising up and taking action, finally having a say in the running of their country. For my uncle, it was an uncertain time that he believed we would all live to regret. Like many others, he thought that Egypt wasn't ready for revolution, nor did it have the infrastructure for democracy. For my mother, it was about the danger this moment posed to her daughter; she wasn't thinking about the outcome. She may have supported the protestors, even agreed with their demands, having grown up in the same broken system. But protecting those she loved was her mission. She would do anything to keep me safe. Just like she had said thank you to the major general all those years ago for Adam's sake, knowing that was the price for his freedom.

I lurched forward as the front wheel of the car sank into a pothole in the road. We were on the bridge heading downtown. I had almost forgotten about the bag of food my uncle had given me that was lodged in between my legs. I thought I should eat it before my hands got too dirty again. I knew that whatever it was, it was likely to be the best meal I'd have for a while.

The container was covered in silver foil and soft pink tissue paper. I opened the lid — expecting to find a chicken or falafel sandwich, something I could eat in the trenches I was heading back to. *I'll probably save some to give my protestor friends in the square*, I thought to myself.

Inside, though, were little, perfect pieces of hand-rolled cucumber-and-avocado sushi, a few strips of fresh pink ginger, and a tiny, clear plastic packet of soy sauce with a smidge of bright-green wasabi on the side. Chopsticks framed the sides of the container.

We were getting closer to Tahrir. From the top of the bridge I heard the familiar sound of thousands shouting, 'The people demand the downfall of the regime,' as the sun set over them.

I resealed the container and hid it on the floor. Like my accent and the driver who opened doors for me, being seen eating sushi would give me away as one of those rich people who handed out their second-hand toys to the poor and then went back to their air-conditioned cars and fancy mansions. The kind that never had to queue for bread. It was the part of my identity I thought it safer to hide. The part I was now afraid the revolutionaries were protesting against.

9.

Angels

Everywhere I went that day, I heard the word *irhal* — 'leave'. Unapologetic. Determined. Bursting from mouths as if teeth were prison bars that had sprung open. The people had been unleashed.

This clear message to the president also now covered most of Tahrir Square. Mounted on cardboard boxes, handwritten on flimsy white pieces of paper, held up by old and determined hands, along with other signs. 'We won't leave until you do.' 'Enough.' 'Free Egypt.' Instructions for the president and signals to the watching world, thousands of them, written in English, Arabic, French, Italian. They were painted on balloons, on the pavements, on the faces of children whose parents had brought them here to witness something never seen before.

Some people spelled their signs backwards — 'so that the president can understand', they wrote, making fun of what they saw as the president's backward thinking. Some used pebbles and rocks to spell out 'FREEDOM' in huge letters. After decades of not being able to question the president's legitimacy, even in your own home, the sight was intoxicating.

We were nine days into the uprising, and tens of thousands of people were now sleeping in Tahrir, vowing to stay until the president stepped down. Women held up photos of sons killed by the Egyptian security forces. The sadness in their eyes had been replaced by hope as they gazed over the crowds — they were not alone, and finally someone was listening.

I approached a woman sitting on her own in the corner, holding a photo of a young man I recognised. Khaled Said was a 28-year-old who had been beaten to death in broad daylight by plain-clothes police on 6 June 2010. His image had become a symbol of the brutality and corruption of the regime. When police tried to claim Khaled had died from choking on a bag of hashish he had in his mouth, the incident sparked national outrage.

'Did you know Khaled?' I asked the woman, crouching down so that I could see her face properly. 'My dear, we are all Khaled Said,' she replied, echoing the slogan that had become common following his death. We sat in silence for a while: the words surrounding us were enough. The protestors' demands, written on a huge white cotton sheet draped from the balcony of an eighth-floor apartment, called for the overthrow of the president, for an end to the state of emergency that had robbed Egyptians of their basic rights for decades, and for members of the regime to be tried. It was signed from 'Egypt's youth'.

The day before, Mubarak had announced he wouldn't seek a sixth presidential term. The gesture was too little and too late, and revealed, yet again, how out of touch the president was. It only made more people come to Tahrir. I had never seen so many Egyptians in one place before. People were singing and dancing, openly discussing politics and making predictions about how long they would have to stay before Mubarak resigned. Young women were walking around, mixing among the crowds with their faces painted red, white, and black, the colours of the Egyptian flag. They walked over the word 'liberty' painted on the ground, for once not having to worry about men catcalling or groping them. There were as many women as men handing out food to the protestors, setting up the tents, talking politics. In the square, the only divide that mattered was whether you were for or against the president.

Just then, I felt a hand on my shoulder. I turned around and looked up to find a stranger holding out his hand. 'I think you dropped this. Take care,' he said, handing me a small yellow purse.

I had left most of my belongings at my uncle's house and was walking around with just my Egyptian ID card and cash. I thanked the man, quickly opening it up to check all the cash my uncle had given me was still inside.

'Is it all there?' the woman beside me said, watching me anxiously count the money. I nodded. She smiled knowingly and started to get up.

'This is the new Egypt — don't be afraid,' she said, as she walked off into a sea of waving flags.

The perimeter of the square was guarded by protestors holding hands, a human chain of resistance. The guards checked identity cards and bags to make sure you weren't undercover police or carrying anything dangerous. They were always friendly, joking as they lightly patted you down.

But that morning was tenser than usual. People had been instructed to drop what they were doing and fortify the chain to protect the square. 'Protection from whom?' I asked a young guy called Amr, an organiser who never seemed to be able to finish a sentence before running off.

'We just got word. Some of Mubarak's thugs are marching on the bridge, heading in our direction. We have to secure the perimeter. Boys! Come on, we need you,' he shouted, tying a bandana around his head. And then Amr was gone.

I grabbed Brad, and we headed for the bridge just a few metres away. As we exited the square, a woman, one of the guards, touched my arm. 'Take care,' she said, the line between her eyebrows deepening. I nodded and ran to catch up with Brad. The Mubarak supporters were nothing like the protestors in Tahrir. They were almost solely young men under 30, shouting pro-government slogans mixed with profanities as they marched, their pupils wide and eyes bulging with rage. For many years, the security forces had dealt with anti-government protests by using what Egyptians called *baltagiya*, hired thugs who dispersed protestors by beating them up. It kept the police out of the spotlight, and made it seem like the president had support. I didn't know who these people were, but there were hundreds of them heading our way, and something told me not to ask them any questions. They probably wouldn't answer a woman, anyway.

Brad filmed as I walked behind him, holding on to his backpack tightly. I usually did this to guide him when we were in big crowds so that he didn't trip over anything. But in truth, I was anxious not to lose him. I didn't want to be left alone with these men.

As the Mubarak supporters crossed the bridge, headed down to Tahrir, I took out my phone and texted Yosra. With the internet still shut down, I had given her my Twitter account details so that she could post for me. Twitter had become one of the main platforms for young people to learn what was going on around the country. Activists and journalists were finding ways around the shutdown to post their updates and tell others what was happening in real time. It was an effective tool for activists to connect the protest movements around Egypt, and letting demonstrators know that they were not alone. For me, it had become the only way to report bits of news quickly, not only to keep our viewers updated when I wasn't on air, but also to inform my own news desk where I was and what I was witnessing when I didn't have a camera. I instructed Yosra to send out a tweet saying that thousands of Mubarak supporters were marching towards Tahrir. She answered right away, telling me that she was watching television and that Al Jazeera was predicting a showdown in the square at any minute.

'Are you sure you should be there?' she asked.

I wasn't, but it was too late to turn back. Brad and I were in the middle of thousands of people, all of them headed towards the square's perimeter with an energy so forceful that trying to move in any other direction was futile. With every step, the crowds around us swelled. People joined from the surrounding streets, carrying sticks and glass bottles. I could see the Tahrir protestors, standing firm and holding hands as the Mubarak supporters cursed at them and threw bottles in their direction, the glass shattering on the ground.

Suddenly, there was no space between us and them. The

Mubarak supporters just in front of me were beating the Tahrir guards with sticks as they tried to get through the cordon. More people were joining from the square, thousands of them running towards the perimeter, climbing over the human chain, colliding with their enemies, determined not to let them in. If the chain broke and the supporters were allowed in, that would surely be the end. People inside would vacate the square and run to safety, releasing the pressure on the president. Ending our revolution.

'Watch out!' Brad shouted at me, as I turned around to find people pushing even more forcefully. They were trying to make space for something just beyond my line of vision. Heads were starting to part, creating a corridor. The shouts were getting louder — I heard cries of *'Allahu Akbar'* as the faces closer to the commotion turned pale, mouths hanging open in shock. And then there they were, two men on horseback, carrying what looked like huge swords. The horses galloped towards us as people tried to get out of their way. But there wasn't enough space, and the men around me starting falling down as others stepped over them, crushing their skulls into the hard pavement below. We were pressed so tightly against each other that I could feel the stomach pulse of the man behind me in my back. The top half of my body was draped almost horizontally against the person in front, and if he moved an inch I would fall; we all would. And then I realised that in the panic I had let go of the strap — I had lost Brad. I started shouting his name, but my voice was drowned out.

Then, out of nowhere, I saw some space. Realising that it must mean the Mubarak supporters had penetrated the square, I thought: *We've lost. I have to run.* I kept telling myself not to fall, reciting, 'I am a tree, I AM A TREE.' If I fell down here, I'd be trampled. I had been trained just to keep going and give in to the flow in situations like this.

The crowds led me to the sides of the square, where a steel fence separated the pavement from the road. My legs were moving at a pace decided by those around me. I knew being near the fence was dangerous because it increased the risk of being crushed, but there was nothing I could do.

Before I had time to think or plan, I had arrived at its big green bars. I held out my arms to stop my body from crashing into them, but it made no difference.

As the front of my body pressed into the hard metal, I felt hands all over my back, my legs, my arms, my hair. I felt my shirt was being lifted and then more hands, now on my skin, grabbing my bra, feeling and groping inside. For a second, I thought this was just part of the stampede; somehow, these hands had become accidentally trapped inside my clothes. I shouted louder and louder, but I couldn't even hear my own voice over the shouts and screams of others around me.

My jeans gave way first, and then the rest of my clothes. The hands were everywhere. I felt moisture on my face: my tears or their sweat, maybe both. I closed my eyes and my strong, stern, angry, loud 'No!' turned into a whispered plea. And then I stopped struggling, giving in to the hands. These cold, rough palms that had found every inch of my body, applying a pressure so intense I felt my bones were being assaulted, too. I closed my eyes, my lips still mouthing, 'No,' as my body relented and muscles softened. There were so many of them, these men, and just one, useless me. It may have lasted only seconds, or maybe minutes. I don't know, because in that moment time, like everything else, didn't matter.

Out of nowhere, a man's hand reached over from the other side of the barrier and grabbed my arm. He lifted me over the bars, my legs flailing, trying to fight off the assailants still tugging at my body from below. Every fibre of my being was trying to get my body over those green bars. A superhuman strength that I can't explain even now was activated, not just in me but in my rescuer, too. I held my breath as I hit the ground on the other side. I was beyond the reach of the hands that had violated me. The man helped me up with one arm, his other wrapped around a young woman who looked injured. I knew that she had seen it all. I turned away, unable to confront her look of sympathy and embarrassment. The man, perhaps her husband, looked at me and said one word: 'Run.'

That was the last I saw of my protector, as he disappeared down one of the side streets. I owe him my life, and wish I could find him, but his face has been completely erased from my memory, as in a powerful dream that dissolves upon waking. I will never be able to thank him for the risk he took, nor identify those who assaulted me. I don't know which is the larger injustice.

I got up and started running until I found a petrol station, a few yards from the square. In my hiding place, crouched behind an old car, I buttoned up my shirt and jeans and wiped my face with my sleeve. My hand was bleeding: I must have caught it on the fence or a piece of broken glass. Now, it began to throb.

My phone vibrated, distracting me from the pain. I reached into my pocket with my good hand and saw a message from Yosra: 'I sent your tweet, hope you're safe now Shusha.' Around me, people were running, but it was unclear from whom, or where they were going. I had to get out of there.

I headed down one of the side streets off the main square, trying to find a way back to my colleagues' hotel. Every side road was blocked by mobs of people, their clothes ripped, fists landing in eyes and stomachs and ribs. Scared residents had hurriedly locked their doors and blockaded the entrances to their buildings with furniture.

Finally, I found a block with an open door and ran up the stairs before anyone saw me. Halfway to the top, on the third or fourth floor, children in their early teens rushed from apartment to apartment. I knocked on one of the half-open doors and saw a child with a big, innocent smile. 'I'm sorry, can I come in for a little while?' I asked. As I spoke, the boy's mother came to the door — looking me up and down while tilting her head in curiosity. 'I was walking downstairs, trying to get home, when I got caught up in all this. I just need somewhere to sit for a few hours if that's okay?' I showed her the cut on my hand. The woman nodded, looking at her son and briefly adopting his smile as she opened the door, allowing me in.

For the next hour, I sat with the family, weaving a careful web of stories about myself — my name was Doris, I was born in London, I went to the American University in Cairo, I studied architecture. I described the gruelling coursework, how I enjoyed living here with my uncle and extended family. I particularly liked the Heliopolis Club near my house, where I played football and ran on the track.

I'd become good at producing these alternative identities on demand. The trick to making stuff up fast, I found, was to base it on someone else's life —only to tell partial lies. That way, you could keep track of the story, and it was easier to believe it

yourself. Doris was my cousin, born in London, who had graduated with an architecture degree from the American University
in Cairo. I'd been to the Heliopolis Club plenty of times, and my
favourite sports were football and running.

It always surprised me how invasive Egyptians could be,
even if they had never met you before. It didn't take long for my
hosts to get to the point. 'Are you married?' the mother asked.
Suddenly, all eyes were on me — even the father, sitting so still in
the corner of the room that I hadn't realised he was there, turned
to look, and the two kids and grandmother also perked up.

'Not yet,' I sighed, feigning regret.

Every now and again we stopped talking and listened to the
television news anchor give an update on the situation. The family
were watching the state television channel. That was the first hint.

'Is it because you're busy with your studies that you're not
married?' asked the mother. There may have been a violent
uprising taking place outside, but that was no reason to get off
the subject of my love life. I tried to think of Doris, but she was
married. I had broken my own rule about not fabricating facts,
and now I had to wing it. As I replied, the news presenter on the
television started to talk about 'Al Jazeera infiltrators' who were
spreading lies about Egypt and trying to embarrass the country
and its people.

Immediately, all three adults started swearing at the
television.

'Those Al Jazeera Islamists are ruining the country!' said the
father.

'They should be arrested and hanged,' echoed the previously
sweet-seeming grandmother.

I understood the feelings of the more hardcore Mubarak supporters from reports I had read, but until then I hadn't actually had a conversation with seemingly ordinary people who simply thought Mubarak didn't deserve to be removed, and that the uprising wasn't a real threat to him. Despite the fact that Tahrir Square was barely 30 yards away from their apartment, this family truly believed what state media was telling them — the protest had been fabricated by Al Jazeera and its Qatari owners to control Egypt. They didn't think the protestors had real grievances, rather that they were a small group of people somehow acting on instructions, the demonstrations around the country orchestrated by a corrupt media determined to stir up turmoil in an otherwise content population.

I had a million questions for them. I wanted to know how they could believe this woman on television, sitting in front of a projected green-screen image of a calm and serene Cairo skyline, when we could hear the running battles below. Their denial was baffling. More than that, it was demoralising. *This is how he will win,* I thought. *This is how Mubarak will be able to reassert his authority.*

I just needed to say as little as possible and keep my head down for the next few hours until things calmed down outside. I quickly reached for my phone, switching it off — the last thing I needed was 'Doha Newsroom' flashing up.

The door to the apartment swung open. A young man, perhaps in his late 20s, rushed in.

'Doris, this is Mahmoud, my eldest son. He is going to America. Mahmoud, speak to Doris in English,' the mother commanded, full of pride.

Mahmoud and I exchanged pleasantries. He spoke English

confidently, telling me that he had learned it mainly from watching television and YouTube videos, which explained his American twang.

'You look familiar to me,' Mahmoud said after a few minutes, looking straight into my eyes as he tried to figure it out. 'Maybe from television.'

I was caught off guard, struggling to come up with a Plan B. I always had a Plan B; if only I could think of what it was. Perhaps Mahmoud had someone else in mind? Yes, that must be it — nobody ever recognised me, especially without my television make-up on.

But my luck had run out. 'Yes! You are that Al Jazeera reporter that was in Gaza with Ayman Mohyeldin! I watched a documentary about you on YouTube,' Mahmoud said excitedly, seemingly unaware of the chaos he had just unleashed.

The words 'Al Jazeera' bounced around the room, and the father was first to react. He stood up so fast I was taken aback.

'You work for Al Jazeera?' he demanded.

I felt the hair on my arms stand up. I denied it, pointing out all the reasons why it was absurd — I was too young to be a reporter, what would I have been doing in Gaza? Also, my Arabic was clearly too poor to work for Al Jazeera or be on television. With that last excuse, I shot a look at Mahmoud. He had got me into this mess; the least he could do was not tell them about English-language Al Jazeera. It was hard to know if I was convincing them, or if they were thinking about throwing me out of the window.

From the corner of my eye, I saw the open door to the bathroom. I leaped towards it, still nattering on, slamming and locking the door behind me. I could hear them outside, mumbling, and more people coming into the apartment as the minutes passed. I had to get out of there. I had my phone in my pocket, but there was no way I could explain where I was, and even if I could, how would anyone get to me? The bathroom window was so dirty I couldn't see out. I twisted the small metal handle and it opened, but not enough for me to be able to climb out, so I forced it all the way, breaking one of the panels. I squeezed my body out on to the fire escape and made my way down the rusty railing, not knowing if the riotous street below was any safer than the lion's den I had just escaped.

I reached the ground and looked back up at the little window. Nobody was there, and I doubted they would risk following me down to the street, where the clashes were still in full force. Among the crowds, I once more searched for a nook to disappear into, as Molotov cocktails lit up the navy-blue sky above me. From all around me came the sounds of men organising themselves, penetrated only by the occasional '*Allahu Akbar*' accompanying the explosion of another home-made bomb.

Just then, I noticed a man standing on his balcony, staring at me intently, more in sorrow than disapproval. I thought he had a kind face. I looked up at him, pleadingly, but he disappeared back into his apartment. I had no idea what to do next, but I found myself reciting the Lord's Prayer: 'Our Father, who art in heaven, hallowed be Thy name.' As I finished the first line, the man reappeared, holding a walking stick almost half his height and motioning with his hand for me to stay where I was.

I did as he indicated and didn't move. The light had now gone completely, and around me thousands of balaclava-clad men were shouting and fighting. They were too busy with their bombs and batons to notice me for now. But that could change at any moment and, remembering my earlier experience, I felt chilled, imagining being trapped here with them until the curfew lifted in the morning.

The man on the balcony emerged from the door of his building after a few minutes, looking smaller and a little older than he did from afar. Gripping the stick firmly in his hands, he crossed the street to get to me, dodging running men.

He introduced himself as Mohamed Essam, adding, 'It's dangerous here; come with me.'

With that, he gripped my arm more tightly than he looked capable of, and we crossed back over the road together, neither of us saying a word. He hadn't asked my name, nor what I was doing climbing down the fire escape of the opposite building. He hadn't asked whose side I was on.

I entered the apartment and saw a woman who I assumed was Mohamed's wife, and a boy perhaps seven years old, sitting on a dirty mattress. There was no other furniture on the wooden boards, which were covered with fraying, dusty prayer mats. A door in one corner led to a small room with a hole in the floor and a dripping tap.

They were eating from a loaf of bread with their hands, breaking it into pieces as if they were going to dip it into something, but instead placing it delicately into their mouths, savouring it as if it was the finest steak. Mohamed split the loaf in half, handing a piece back to his son and another to me. 'I can't take all of this,' I said, walking towards the mattress. But he insisted, 'You need it. Allah will provide for my family.'

I sat down outside on the balcony and ate. I was starving; I hadn't eaten a proper meal since my uncle's house. As I chewed my food, a pain from my pelvis shot into my stomach and I winced, catching myself before letting out a full cry. I knew what it was. My insides had been contracting like that for hours.

My phone was vibrating again. This time, it was Ayman.

'They've won,' he said bluntly, before describing what was happening outside, how the Mubarak supporters were trying to storm Tahrir by encircling it with cars, dumpsters, and steel road signs they had torn down. Ayman sounded agitated and tired. Where had all these people come from? We both knew they were not spontaneously coming to the defence of their beloved president. Rather, it seemed like a coordinated attack by a desperate regime.

I told Ayman that because of the curfew I would be stuck on Mohamed's balcony until sunrise. It was a miracle that Mohamed had found me and taken me in: this small man with enormous strength.

My mother had told me growing up that when she prayed for me, she wasn't asking God to keep danger away. 'It's inevitable that you'll be in trouble sometimes, you more than most people!' she joked. Rather, she prayed for God to send me an angel when I needed one. At the time, I had nodded politely and smiled at her when she said such things, a little jealous of her unquestioning faith.

I didn't know whether in the moment when Mohamed left his apartment to come and get me, he had had any doubts about the wisdom of his actions. All I knew was that when he told me to follow him, I didn't hesitate. I was struck with a strong feeling, for the second time that day, that someone had been sent to help me.

Looking back from the balcony, I saw Mohamed and his family sleeping peacefully on the mattress, surrounded by bread-crumbs. The small boy's head was buried in his mother's chest, a leg draped over his father's stomach. I lowered my head until it met the cement floor and closed my eyes, surprised by how easy it felt to let everything go, despite the battle cries below. Ayman had promised to get me when the curfew lifted. All I had to do now was wait for morning.

10.

Take Back Your Square, Take Back Your Country

When I woke up on the floor of the balcony the next morning, my entire body throbbed. The rising sun made it impossible to ignore the dried blood on my hand, bruises on my chest and ribs, and the shooting pain in my abdomen.

Ayman arrived and took me back to his apartment, where I showered. I scrubbed myself violently with the rough loofah and hot water until my body turned different shades of red, and I could hardly tell the bruises from the normal patches of skin.

Wrapping myself in an oversized towel, I sat on the sofa in the living room, hair dripping on to the parquet floor. The sun glimmered through the still-drawn curtains. Ayman asked me what had happened the night before and how I had got all those bruises, but I didn't say a word.

The body is programmed to repair itself; bruises fade as the blood under the skin breaks down, broken bones knit back together and become whole again. But though the body heals, it never forgets. It will do everything in its power to ensure it won't be hurt in the same way again. At the merest hint of a returning threat, it will send a rush of powerful hormones to quicken the heart, sensing danger where it never did before. It will remember, even when you don't want it to, even when your brain has managed to push the memory of what happened so deep into your unconscious that you're not even sure it happened anymore.

My body continued to remind me of that night for many years. Every time I was in a large crowd of people, every time I felt a cold hand on my bare skin or the intense smell of a man's sweat mixed with cologne. Every time kissing a boyfriend seemed like it was leading to something more. My reactions varied: sometimes I just held my breath or dug my nails into the palm of my hand; other times I ran to the bathroom and threw up. But it was there, all the time, forcing me to make up stories for why I was the way I was.

It took a long time to forgive myself for not fighting harder against the men who assaulted me. To understand why I froze in those crucial seconds when my body was pressed against the green bars, and then just minutes later acted as though nothing had happened, sitting in a room talking politely with strangers, watching their television. How I spoke to multiple people and texted Yosra and my mother in the middle of it all without a hint that anything was wrong. How I went on air and gave live updates from Mohamed's balcony late that same night. How I slept soundly on his floor and dreamed of nothing.

Every time I thought about telling someone what had happened to me, a voice in my head told me not to, because I would have to explain my behaviour and why I didn't say anything at the time. I wouldn't be able to answer those questions. The more time that passed, the harder it got to speak up. Surely my actions that night were not those of a normal victim? I had no evidence anything had happened, and there were no witnesses, at least not any that I could identify. Perhaps nobody would even believe me.

When I finally opened up about my assault years later and told my friend and colleague Tamara Bralo, she listened and never once doubted me. At the end of my story, as I continued to question my own reactions that night, she took my hand and said, 'If only you accepted how strong you are, it would all make much more sense to you.' She wasn't just talking about me. In so many cases, a sexual assault victim's instinct to survive can make their story less believable.

It's unlikely that I was the only one assaulted near Tahrir that night. We know that at least eight cases of assault were reported around Cairo over the course of the uprising. The most well-known survivor was the CBS News correspondent Lara Logan, who spoke out about how she was brutally beaten and raped by a gang of men using sticks and flagpoles. She was rescued by a group of Egyptian women and soldiers and hospitalised for days. Sadly, many more women were probably attacked like I was during the protests, but did not report the incidents, perhaps because they were ashamed, or because they knew it wouldn't lead to anyone being held accountable. Perhaps they even feared reprisals from the authorities. I would later learn from activist friends how sexual harassment and assault in Egypt are a major public threat against women, with nine out of ten Egyptian women having experienced assault in some form. What happened to me that night near Tahrir was simply the tip of the iceberg. The sad truth is that even had I reported it at the time, it would likely never have been investigated, much less led to any of those involved being caught or prosecuted.

———

The mob vanished just as quickly as it had appeared. They had fought all night to gain ground, but the protestors had stood firm, and by the early hours of the morning, most of Mubarak's supporters had given up and returned home. By noon, the square and surrounding streets were back in the hands of the protestors. The women and men came back in huge numbers with their tents and belongings, cleaning the streets, picking up broken bottles, and dismantling the barriers that had formed the front lines of the night before. 'We are taking back our square, taking back our country,' they shouted, more determined than ever.

The protestors reinforced the perimeters of the square. There were now even more checks to get inside, with more people guarding the makeshift entrances. Tahrir once more felt safe and came back to life, re-energising those who were beginning to lose hope. Meanwhile, national strikes were bringing the country to a halt. Mubarak responded by offering a few concessions that only served to show the protestors that he was not yet taking them seriously.

On the morning of 10 February, word spread that the president was going to address the nation that evening. Commentators on television speculated that he would step down. The mood in the square was one of sheer elation — fighter jets were flying over Tahrir, and protests everywhere swelled to numbers not seen since the very first days of the uprising. Local and international media reported that a meeting of the Military Council had taken place, which had excluded both President Mubarak and his vice-president, Omar Suleiman, sparking rumours of a military takeover. US officials from the Obama administration began publicly signalling the need for a transition. Even the head of the ruling party — the president's own party — said that Mubarak should go, for the good of the country. The president was losing support within and outside Egypt, and it was hard to see how he could remain in power.

The only official insisting that Mubarak was not stepping down that night was the information minister, Anas el-Fiqqi. Few believed el-Fiqqi, seeing his denial as the desperate act of a regime on its last legs. But if anyone knew the contents of Mubarak's speech that night, it would have been his minister of information.

My uncle suspected el-Fiqqi was right. He called to warn me not to be near the square when the announcement was being made.

'I'm not telling you this to broadcast, I'm telling you to be careful because the protestors will be angry when they realise he is not going,' my uncle reasoned. 'I can't explain this to you right now, but the military are playing games; they are not ready to cut Mubarak loose yet.'

We had barely spoken since I had had lunch with him at the

house. I had promised to take care that day and not to take risks — that had been the condition of my release. He had warned me not to underestimate how dangerous the streets were. But I had broken my promise, and paid a price.

'I won't go to the square today,' I said to my uncle, stopping him in mid-sentence. He stayed quiet, as if wondering whether to believe me. I wasn't arguing or saying '*Insha'Allah*' to get him off my back. He wished me luck and hung up the phone. I knew that this could be the moment we were all waiting for, the big resignation. All the other reporters would be jockeying to be in Tahrir for the announcement. But not me. I didn't want to be around crowds of people, even if it was to film them celebrating, even on what could be an historic day. My body tensed just thinking about it. I didn't need to explain my decision to my editors; they simply assumed I was exhausted.

Instead, I went on my own to a cafe in a nearby neighbourhood called Zamalek to watch the announcement on television with other Egyptians. The cafe was close to Ayman's apartment, just across the river from Tahrir Square. Zamalek has some of the capital's most iconic cultural landmarks. It's where rich Egyptians and tourists mix with ordinary people on narrow one-way streets, where lovers find small, hidden corners along the Nile to hold hands and steal quick kisses.

I sat at one of the smaller cafes along the main street, relieved to be offduty for the night. This wasn't where the rich kids went for their shisha and tea; there were no lattes or comfortable sofas surrounded by fake IKEA plants. Here, there were only two things on the menu — black tea or Turkish coffee. Whichever you chose would come in a vessel not much bigger than a shot glass, and be placed on a rickety table. The people in this cafe came to drink, smoke, and play backgammon while a barely working fan above them shooed the flies away. The shisha was cheap and the conversation endless.

By the time Mubarak started speaking, I could barely see the television for all the smoke in the room. The customers fell silent, the dice still in their hands, as they looked up at the president's face filling the small screen in the corner of the shop.

As my uncle had predicted, Mubarak didn't step down that evening. He was merely offering to stay until the end of his term later in the year and not seek re-election. It took several minutes for the people in the cafe to realise this was not the resignation speech they were expecting. Almost immediately, I could hear crowds outside the cafe gathering and a furious chant rising: 'Down with the regime!'

The protestors interviewed on television said they felt the president had insulted them for the last time. Mohamed ElBaradei, an Egyptian Nobel Peace Prize laureate and former head of the UN nuclear watchdog, had joined the protests. He offered to lead a transitional government, declaring that 'Egypt will explode' as a result of Mubarak's actions.

In the cafe, conversation was getting louder. Arguments broke out about what the announcement meant, and whether the president had offered enough concessions. The majority opinion was that he had not, but that he was now on the way out. One man, who was loosely defending the president, or perhaps just complaining about the protests, was shouted down by the others. He sat back and took a long drag of his shisha while mumbling that Egyptians were never happy.

The next day, 11 February, was dubbed the 'Friday of Departure' by the opposition, as increasingly massive protests swelled in cities around Egypt. In Cairo, the demonstrations reached the doors of the presidential palace.

Twenty-four hours after Mubarak's television appearance, Vice-President Omar Suleiman appeared in front of the nation looking solemn and defeated. In a statement that lasted 30 seconds, he announced that the president had decided to step down after three decades in power.

He ended his address saying, 'May God help us all.'

Mubarak and his family were flown to a military base and then to their holiday residence in the seaside town of Sharm el-Sheikh. An army council was now in charge of the country, an interim arrangement to last until there was a full transition of power. ElBaradei, an opposition figure who was emerging as a possible presidential candidate, declared that Egypt was now free.

As the news spread, hundreds of thousands of people left their homes to celebrate, waving the Egyptian flag and shouting *'Tahya Misr'* — 'Long live Egypt.' The energy in the streets was like nothing I had witnessed, born of a hope that had never before existed. The army withdrew the next day with crowds cheering them out, throwing roses at the tanks and blowing kisses at the soldiers. Protestors returned to Tahrir as victorious citizens, and for the next few days they cleaned and scrubbed the streets. Old and young, rich and poor, Muslim and Christian, they came holding huge black garbage bags, singing and smiling as they picked up trash with their bare hands. This was their country now.

I had feared a change in mood after Mubarak's fall, a turn against the upper classes and those who were seen to have been allied with the president. But there was no such feeling in the square. It was as if everyone was united in feeling responsible for a country that was new and vulnerable. The revolution had no leader, no person who had claimed to represent the masses against authoritarian rule. It was at once everybody's, and nobody's.

Suleiman's announcement that Mubarak had stepped down was like a universal summons for journalists. They arrived in their dozens from all over the globe, and within days, hundreds of foreign correspondents were travelling around the country. Every hour brought new and unprecedented developments that needed to be captured for the watching eyes of the world.

As it had during the Gaza War, Al Jazeera English was having a moment in the spotlight, enjoying a spike in the number of viewers and turning ordinary reporters into overnight celebrities. *Vanity Fair* ran a piece called 'Waking the Lion' about the revolutionaries who had defied death to get rid of Mubarak, featuring a full-page photo of me taken at the Nile Hilton Hotel, phone in hand as I talked about building democracy.

I was the only journalist in the piece; the rest of the individuals profiled were activists. It felt like an honour to be alongside them. In fact, in the days following Mubarak's ousting, I found I had very little interest in reporting on events. Instead, I wanted to walk through Tahrir, sit on the grassy area in the middle where the tents used to be, and inhale the sense of victory. I had no desire to tell the story. I wanted to live it.

Years of studying and reporting on conflicts in the Middle

East had made me believe that people in the region were destined to live under a system of oppression. This was our for ever fight. I had covered protests in Egypt, Jerusalem, Lebanon — and with each one I had grown more convinced that little changed in this region. Not really, not for long.

But in the haze of post-Mubarak bliss, anything seemed possible. My faith in Egyptians to create a different narrative grew with every flag I saw waving. There was no denying that we were heading into the unknown: most of us had not known anything but Mubarak's 30-year rule. But the protestors were going into it willingly, having chosen this path.

I saw my uncle's number light up on my phone.

'See what happened?' he said, considerably less excited than those around me.

'Yes, it's amazing! I can't believe he's gone.'

But my uncle was not happy. 'No, I mean did you see that the military issued a statement, called *communiqué number one* — saying they have formed a supreme council to deal with the running of the country,' he said, sighing. 'Does this sound like a transition to civilian rule to you? You don't know the military. They are powerful, and the revolutionaries have no idea how to run a country. This is a mess.'

With that, my uncle hung up.

He sounded afraid. Perhaps he wasn't sure if his friends in the military would continue to protect him and the family. Perhaps he was scared of change and the inevitable uncertainty it brings.

But he hadn't seen what I had these past few weeks, I reasoned. The kindness and solidarity. The determination that under the new order everyone's human rights and freedoms should be respected. These were not people turning on each other, but ones who wanted a fairer system for all.

Whichever one of us was right, we'd find out in the months to come. But for today, I just wanted to celebrate the undeniable feeling that the people had won.

11.

The Other Side

There's not always a clear line between journalism and activism. When you're working under an authority intent on restricting human rights, the distinction becomes even cloudier. Lebanon, Gaza, Egypt — they taught me that there weren't always two, equally weighted, sides to every story. Sometimes, one side was just right. Although I never subscribed to, and neither did Al Jazeera adhere to, the notion of journalism simply as giving the facts and allowing the viewer to decide, there was still a difference between presenting a situation in an informed light and actively choosing a side by lobbying for changes in policy. In other words, while I was clearly reporting that the departure of President Hosni Mubarak was a euphoric and positive moment for Egypt, I wasn't personally devoting myself to ensuring the country was building democratic institutions and espousing liberal values. That, for me, wasn't my mandate. That was crossing the line.

For some, though, journalism was deeply wrapped in a larger agenda that was unapologetically driven by activism. This was the case for my boyfriend, whom I met in Cairo shortly after I moved there for AJE, following Mubarak's downfall. We had both initially been sent by our respective media outlets to cover the revolution, and then became personally invested in the events that unfolded. He was also Egyptian and had spent most of his life living in the West, in his case in the United States. Our connection was easy and organic, both of us straddling two different worlds, each trying to reconcile our family's class and privilege with our ideals of what a just and equal society should look like. He had struggled with his identity growing up in a similar way to the way I did, and his Egyptian family also made fun of his accent when he spoke in Arabic. He understood about being a *halfie*. It also helped that he was both very handsome and charmingly unaware of this fact. His stubbled beard gave him a rock-and-roll air, while his round, slightly droopy brown eyes and untameable curls made him sweet and unintimidating.

After a few weeks of chatting at parties and meeting for coffees, he offered to cook me dinner at his apartment, but then locked himself out when he left to buy the food. He called me in a panic, and we ended up talking on the phone for hours while he sat outside the door waiting for the locksmith, surrounded by shopping bags. I was taken by his sincerity; he spoke about Egyptian politics, his upbringing, and his journey to journalism with vulnerability and warmth. The next evening, I went over to his place and we ate and talked more until the sun came up. I walked home in a daze that morning, admiring the brightly coloured houseboats that lined the River Nile. Cairo had never looked so beautiful.

RIGHT: My parents, Ihab and Sylvia, moments after my father proposed in London's famous Trafalgar Square. My mother was still living in Egypt and my father was showing her around the sights, hoping she would fall in love with the city. She did, and with him. *Author's collection, 1974*

Queen Elizabeth 2

Photographed on board 1984

LEFT: My father loved taking us on trips to visit new countries. In 1984, we sailed to Fort Lauderdale, Florida on the *Queen Elizabeth 2* (*QE2*). It was the first time any of us had been to America. I could never have imagined back then that one day I'd move there. *Author's collection, 1984*

BELOW: My fondest childhood memories are of holidays in Cairo with my siblings. We grew even closer when in Egypt, perhaps because we often felt like foreigners amongst my Egyptian cousins. *Sylvia Tadros, 1985*

LEFT: I'm around six years old here, with my parents and aunt Mira, during a summer holiday in the South of France. My family found it very amusing when I mispronounced Arabic words, which I frequently did. See my mother's reaction after one such blunder, and her comforting hold. *Hoda Ayad, 1986*

RIGHT: My maternal grandmother Hoda, whom we called Doudou, at home in Cairo. She was always well dressed even if she wasn't going out, a habit my mother inherited. *Ihab Tadros, 1987*

LEFT: On the first night of the Gaza war, with Al Jazeera Arabic producer Wessam Hammad. When the strikes began, he taped the letters 'TV' on all the windows of our office to try to signal to Israeli forces not to bomb our building. *Ayman Mohyeldin, 2008*

RIGHT: Taken while reporting on the massacre of a Palestinian family called the Samounis during the Gaza war. Family members told me they'd been trapped inside their homes for days amidst shelling and missile strikes, surrounded by the dead bodies of their relatives. *Ayman Mohyeldin, 2009*

RIGHT: In Gaza with my crew, surveilling the damage after a ceasefire was declared. Entire neighbourhoods were flattened and roads destroyed to the point where some residents had to use horses to reach their homes. Once they did, some found that Israeli soldiers had left empty tins of food on the floor or written racist slurs on the walls in Arabic. *Ayman Mohyeldin, 2009*

BELOW: Ayman took this at one of our favorite places in occupied East Jerusalem, the Austrian Hospice in the Old City. From the rooftop you can see some of the holiest sites of the three major monotheistic religions. *Ayman Mohyeldin, 2009*

LEFT: Me with my childhood friend Yosra, following a grueling reporting stint in Palestine. We met up in London, at our favorite lunch spot in Baker Street, just next to where we went to school together. She insisted I needed a hug and told me not to believe the story in my head about having to be tough. I miss her every day. *Dina Selim, 2010*

BELOW: Dressed up at the International Emmy Awards, where Ayman and I were nominated for our 2008–9 Gaza coverage. By then, the war seemed to be a distant memory and the news cycle had moved on to other stories. *Author's collection, 2010*

BELOW: Covering the Egyptian uprising remains the highlight of my career as a journalist. This image captures the excitement and energy in Cairo's Tahrir Square as protestors spoke honestly, without fear, about the regime. *Kim Badawi, 2011*

ABOVE: As a reporter, you ask people to trust you with their stories, and it's not always easy to convince them to speak, especially in oppressive environments. During and immediately after the fall of Egyptian President Hosni Mubarak, there was an atmosphere of hope. Sadly, it didn't take long before a state of fear and repression returned to the streets. *Omar Fouad, 2011*

RIGHT: Protests in Tahrir Square continued after President Mubarak was ousted. This photo of me and Al Jazeera cameraman Omar Fouad was taken in Tahrir almost one year after Mubarak fell. *Max Becherer, 2012*

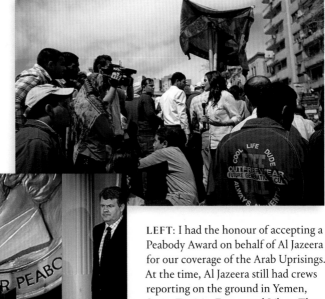

LEFT: I had the honour of accepting a Peabody Award on behalf of Al Jazeera for our coverage of the Arab Uprisings. At the time, Al Jazeera still had crews reporting on the ground in Yemen, Syria, Tunisia, Egypt, and Libya. That is what set Al Jazeera apart from other networks — its commitment to the story long after others left. *Peabody, 2012*

LEFT: A big part of broadcast television is finding the perfect place to go live from. Here I am reporting on the protests against Egyptian President Mohamed Morsi, from the roof of our van. I'm smiling at France 24 correspondent and friend Sonia Dridi. The colleagues I met during my journalism days remain the best and most loyal friends I have today. *Sonia Dridi, 2012*

RIGHT: We travelled to Tunisia to investigate why so many Tunisians were joining the Islamic State group. One of our interviewees was a former member of the group, who told us his motive for joining, like so many of his friends, was financial rather than ideological. *Zein Ja'Far, 2015*

BELOW: By 2015, the Iraqi military were on a mission to show the world that they had the upper hand in the fight against the Islamic State group. They organised for us to travel in an Iraqi army helicopter to Anbar Province, western Iraq, where they were starting to push the terrorists back. *Zein Ja'Far, 2015*

ABOVE: Shortly after leaving journalism for advocacy in the summer of 2017, I gave a press conference about the Myanmar military's brutal attack on the Rohingya people in Rakhine State. My colleague Tirana Hassan spoke, via videolink from Bangladesh, of the horrific stories she was hearing from people fleeing, especially from the women. *Mike Navallo, 2017*

ABOVE: A United Nations press conference was called after the brazen murder of Saudi journalist Jamal Khashoggi at the Saudi consulate in Istanbul. I represented Amnesty and joined forces with colleagues from Human Rights Watch and the Committee to Protect Journalists to demand the UN launch an investigation. The continued lack of justice in this case underscores the failure to punish killers of journalists around the world. *Getty Images, 2018*

RIGHT: Activism is about coming up with creative ways to grab people's attention, and this is one I'm most proud of. During the UN General Assembly, we stuck 'wanted' posters of Min Aung Hlaing, the Burmese general responsible for the ethnic cleansing of the Rohingya, on the pavement around the UN Headquarters. Amnesty Secretary-General at the time, Kumi Naidoo, is seen here with a colleague, almost stepping on the general's face. *Author's collection, 2018*

BELOW: Speaking alongside then CNN Senior Correspondent Arwa Damon in Washington DC about journalism and human rights. *Center for Strategic and International Studies, 2019*

BELOW: This was the first time I spoke in the UN General Assembly Hall since the outbreak of the pandemic. I criticised the UN for continuing to block civil society access to the building, even after COVID-19 restrictions were lifted for all other passholders. Protecting the space for human rights defenders' voices to be heard, whether at the UN or in countries like Egypt, continues to be one of my most challenging and important missions. *Louis Charbonneau, 2022*

Within weeks, we were spending all our free time together. My colleagues would catch me randomly smiling while thinking about him and remark how much happier I seemed since we had started dating. The best part of my day was meeting him after work at the cafe near my office. I'd look up at him and think, *I can't believe he's really mine.*

We also went on holiday together, visiting Yosra in New York a few times, where she was still trying to make it as a photographer. We shared reporting trips around Egypt, as well as to Yemen and other countries that were experiencing uprisings as had Egypt and Tunisia. He was a founding member of and reporter for an independent American broadcast news show. The channel never shied away from its agenda to promote democratic ideals and peace in all countries. The host, an award-winning journalist, was known for being outspoken and anti-establishment. She had been arrested along with my boyfriend, who was her producer at the time, during anti-war protests in 2008 — an incident that quickly earned them both a certain notoriety.

This was a new breed of journalist, unafraid of telling their audience what they believed in. When I was starting out in journalism, it was considered a slur to be called an activist. It meant that you had broken the sacred vow of neutrality. But things were changing.

My boyfriend never hesitated before sending a tweet supporting a political candidate or using explicit language to describe leaders he thought were oppressing their citizens. Sometimes he would go to protests and join the demonstrators calling for political change. He was of the school of thought that there was no such thing as a journalist without opinions, only those who pretended not to have them. It made me question my less partisan approach. By holding back in the name of neutrality, was I just being dishonest with my audience? I didn't always agree with or even understand his journalism, but I admired his honesty and commitment. It helped that he was a good writer, blending politics and emotion with poetic ease.

Soon, I was barely spending any time in my own apartment anymore and so, without much thought, we moved in together. So much was happening politically in the post-uprising world that there was barely time to discuss anything personal. We were happy in our one-bedroom apartment in Zamalek, overlooking the River Nile, near Ayman's house and surrounded by other journalists and activists of similar ages and opinions to us. One of our closest friends was Leila Fadel, then a reporter for *The Washington Post*. Leila was Lebanese American and had spent many years covering the war in Iraq before moving to Cairo. We had met through Ayman during the protests, the morning before Tahrir Square was stormed by Mubarak's supporters. The first time I saw her she was on the phone with her editor, hair gathered in a loose bun on the top of her head as she paced around her pen-scattered hotel room. Even in that moment, she was caring: her first words to me were, 'You look thirsty — I'll get you some water.'

In our tiny, tight-knit, *halfie* news bubble, we covered stories of post-Mubarak Egypt — from the narrow victory of the Muslim Brotherhood, an Islamist movement, in the country's first democratic elections, to a *coup d'état* the following year, in which Field Marshal Abdel Fattah el-Sisi removed the new president, Mohamed Morsi, from office. One of the most harrowing events came just after Morsi was ousted, when over 900 anti-coup protestors, mainly supporters of the Muslim Brotherhood, were killed by police during a sit-in. The raid was later described by rights groups as constituting crimes against humanity. Throughout Egypt's supposed democratisation after Mubarak's ouster, the military had lurked in the background. The leaderless nature of the revolution had gone from being a beautiful expression of the people's will to an ugly and chaotic mess. Those who had spent decades amassing power were still pulling the strings.

Getting rid of Mubarak had been as ineffective as cutting the head off a Hydra — no sooner had one tyrant been deposed than another one instantly threatened to appear in its place. Below Mubarak sat deep and tangled networks of oppressive institutions that had yet to be dismantled, including the military and the interior ministry. Perhaps that was what Uncle Ayad had been trying to warn me of that day when we were celebrating in Tahrir Square. Removing Mubarak was not the same as ending the regime that had made him.

The relentlessness with which events were unfolding in Egypt made it feel like we were covering a protracted war. Every day saw new developments and urgent, breaking news. It was exhilarating, but also depressing and exhausting. By the middle of 2013, a counter-revolution was in full force, and the old guard, led by el-Sisi, was out for revenge. First on their target list was the opposition party that had taken power after Mubarak left office — the Muslim Brotherhood. There was little sympathy for the Brotherhood among the population at large. Their short time in office under President Morsi had been spent trying to consolidate their power by enacting reforms that proved unpopular with young revolutionaries and deeply worried the country's Christian minority, including my own family. After the massacre at the sit-in, hundreds of Brotherhood members were being rounded up by the regime and thrown in jail. They were tried en masse without due process, and many of them were sentenced to death, including former president Mohamed Morsi. My boyfriend's uncle was a member of the Muslim Brotherhood and a vocal opposition figure. He lived in fear for months, but thankfully was never taken by the police.

The other targets of the regime were the free press and human rights defenders. Foreign journalists were being harassed by the police at every opportunity, often accused of being spies. Under Mubarak, Al Jazeera had been considered enemy number one, a position we were swiftly returning to now. Local journalists who dared speak out were arrested in their homes and detained. Activists were surveilled and harassed, and those were the lucky ones. Every so often, we would hear of someone disappearing on their way to work, only to find out weeks or months later that they had been held incommunicado, cut off from the outside world and denied access to a lawyer. Some suffered beatings and abuse to extract confessions for the authorities to use against them in trials. Like the rest of my colleagues, I lived in fear of arrest. I kept my lawyer's number on speed dial and had a detailed plan for who would do what in case I was detained. My colleagues and friends checked in with each other every night to make sure nobody had been taken.

Human rights investigators from Amnesty International and Human Rights Watch were dispatched to Cairo, where they reported a massive crackdown on free speech by the state. Two years after the uprising, and tens of thousands of political prisoners were being jailed, many without charge, and subjected to the exact same kind of inhumane conditions and torture that we had seen under Mubarak. I thought about the prison cells I had seen when I reported from Abu Zaabel, their smell of rotten food mixed with human waste, and the hard cement floors where inmates had been forced to sleep. The prisons that had been emptied during the uprising were now being populated again with those who dared to oppose the new military regime. The prisoners I had interviewed at Abu Zaabel that day had been sceptical in a way I could not understand at the time. They had predicted this day of reckoning because they had seen first-hand the wrath of the deep state.

The rapid deterioration of human rights and freedoms in a country where there had been a moment of real hope was difficult to comprehend, let alone accept. It was one thing when nothing was changing in Egypt, quite another to witness the situation worsen in this dramatic way. I felt embarrassed that I had read the situation so wrong, that I had stood in Tahrir Square on the day Mubarak stepped down and called it historic on television.

I could no longer predict where the country was headed. After so much tumult, it felt as though even the people were slowly accepting the return of an oppression that at least felt familiar to them. At one point, during a live interview about el-Sisi announcing a low-profile judge called Adly Mansour as the country's new interim president, the presenter asked me a question about what was likely to happen next. 'I don't know,' I replied. 'I threw my crystal ball in the River Nile months ago.'

I was bitter, and it was starting to show in my reporting. As much as I was enjoying my new relationship and the circle of friends that made Cairo feel like home, the situation was becoming increasingly dangerous and especially depressing for those of us who had been expecting things to change after Mubarak's ouster. But the political turmoil in Egypt wasn't the only thing in my life I felt powerless and angry about.

My friend Yosra had finally got her big career break in New York — a job taking photos for Beyoncé. She would call me after her long workdays and tell me crazy stories about hanging out with the singer and her family at home, and how much fun she was having. One time, as Yosra was taking photos of Beyoncé shooting a video, the singer stopped and asked her if she could borrow the sneakers she was wearing because she thought they looked cool — Yosra was so flattered, she could barely respond. She called that day, squealing with delight. 'She thought *my* sneakers were cool! Can you believe it?'

But soon after that, while on Beyoncé's world tour, Yosra started to feel very tired and was having trouble swallowing. We assumed it was exhaustion from all the hard work and excitement. During a stop in London, the crew's doctor suggested Yosra see a specialist. Within days, she was told she had inoperable, stage-four oesophageal cancer and had to start treatment immediately, which meant quitting the tour and staying in London.

After her diagnosis, I spent the next few months flying in from Cairo to visit her while she underwent regular chemotherapy. I went with her when she decided to take control over what was happening to her body and shave off what was left of her hair. She said she wanted to do it while she still had some long strands left, so that she could donate it to a charity that made wigs for kids with cancer. It was all happening so fast, but we stayed positive, and I visited her in London as often as I could, spending nights eating popcorn and watching reruns of *Friends* on the television, just like we did at Number 29 when we were kids.

———

By late 2013, it had become impossible to report for Al Jazeera from Egypt safely. I was feeling like more of a bystander than ever before, watching events unfold and yet hesitant even to report what was happening for fear of reprisals from the regime. The authorities were watching Al Jazeera closely for any sign we were stirring up anti-regime sentiment. They wouldn't grant us permits to cover events or film on the streets, and if we said something on air they didn't like, we would be 'invited' to the government press centre and given a stern talking-to about the importance of reporting 'the truth', followed by multiple calls from unknown numbers imparting the same advice.

Finally, just before Christmas, I resigned from AJE. I didn't have another job lined up. The British broadcaster Sky News had reached out to see if I was interested in setting up a bureau for them in Cairo, but I had decided I wanted to try going freelance, thinking that could give me more freedom to report and also to travel when I needed to.

A few weeks after returning from a trip to see Yosra in late December 2013, I met up with Ayman, who was now a Cairo-based correspondent for MSNBC. We were having dinner when both our phones lit up with a breaking news alert: 'Three Al Jazeera English reporters arrested.' We looked up at each other, and I felt the hair on my arms stand on end, just as it had on the first day of the war in Gaza. I called my boyfriend to check on him, while Ayman called our good friend Rawya Rageh, a correspondent with AJE who had also covered the revolution and subsequent events in Egypt. Rawya was one of those journalists who had sources everywhere and always seemed to know what was going on before the rest of us. We found out that the police had raided the hotel room where AJE had set up base — the previous weeks had been so dangerous for them that the crew had moved to the Marriott Hotel — close to where Ayman and I were having dinner. Mohamed Fahmy, an Egyptian Canadian producer formerly with CNN, along with our Egyptian producer Baher Mohamed, and Peter Greste, an Australian correspondent newly arrived in the country, were all now in detention.

While I filled my boyfriend in about what we were hearing, my phone started to beep. It was my mother on call waiting. She had just seen the alert. 'Are you okay?' she blurted out.

'Yes, yes, I'm fine. It's Mohamed, Baher, and Peter,' I informed her. I had only recently quit AJE; it could so easily have been me in that hotel room.

'God help them,' she kept repeating, relieved but aware of how serious this was for our colleagues.

Despite predictions that the arrests were just a warning by the regime to the foreign press, and that the men would soon be released, the three of them were thrown in jail. They were charged with affiliation to the Muslim Brotherhood, which had been designated a terrorist organisation, and with 'fabricating footage to undermine Egypt's national security'. Peter Greste, who had never before been to Egypt and did not speak Arabic, was treated like the others and thrown in a cell in Cairo's Tora

Prison. After months behind bars and a sham trial, he and Fahmy were sentenced to seven years in prison, and our Egyptian producer, Baher, was sentenced to ten. The verdicts prompted outrage from across the world. Fifty global news organisations, along with world leaders, called for the men's immediate release.

Now I was freelance and not associated with any news network, I could finally be more of an activist without getting reprimanded by my bosses or colleagues for crossing the line. I felt like I had entered a world that had previously been off limits. I started organising and advocating for the release of my three colleagues, alongside their friends and families. Together, we wrote letters to politicians, arranged prison visits, and held meetings with officials in Cairo, including the head of the foreign press centre and an advisor to Abdel Fattah el-Sisi, who had just been elected president. I helped gather the signatures of well-known journalists, including Christiane Amanpour, calling for the men's release and declaring that 'journalism is not a crime' — a hashtag which was soon trending, thanks to AJE's campaign. As hopeless as the situation was, there were moments when I felt the resulting pressure on the regime was making a difference. Sometimes, it led to an extra prison visit for the detainees, or allowed them to send a letter to their families. After the arrest, police had raided Baher Mohamed's home, terrorising his wife and child and even shooting his dog. Baher was desperate to find out how his family were doing, and letters were often the only way to communicate with him — including letting him know that his dog was still alive.

I was in contact with Baher's wife, visiting her and their son at home while Baher was in prison. One morning, she called me, distraught, after hearing that Baher was in excruciating pain because one of his teeth was rotting and he desperately needed to see a dentist. I immediately called some of the other activists involved in Baher's case, and we set up a meeting with an Egyptian official known to have sway with the head of Tora Prison, where the men were detained. Eventually, Baher was allowed to receive treatment. We may not have done enough to convince President el-Sisi and his regime to release the men, but officials lower down the chain were increasingly uneasy about the bad press the regime was getting worldwide as a result of our campaign.

An official even allowed us to watch from outside the prison as Baher was transported to his dentist's appointment. Ironically, the last time I had seen him, we had been filming a story together about the family of a wrongfully imprisoned protestor. Baher was young and handsome, with big green eyes; usually he had a smile on his face, but now he looked exhausted. As I watched him get into the car, wearing prison overalls and looking frail, I thought about that shoot and how even then Baher had known how dangerous his work was, warning me that any one of us could be next in this senseless crackdown.

———

The jailing of my colleagues, and my advocacy on their behalf, had made it difficult to travel to see Yosra as often as I wanted. And as the situation deteriorated in Egypt, so too did Yosra's condition. The chemotherapy slowly stopped working, outpaced by the cancer that was ravaging her body.

At 32, she had never smoked or drunk alcohol; she worked out and was otherwise completely healthy. We knew the statistics were not in her favour, but she was just so young, and being told that there were no other treatments we could try, or clinical trials available, felt like an unbelievable blow. Yosra's brother would update me on how she was doing, and she and I would speak on the phone on the good days when she had more energy. Despite everything she was going through, Yosra remained upbeat and hopeful, determined to keep fighting. She said that given nobody could have predicted that someone her age would get oesophageal cancer, why was it far-fetched to believe she could beat the odds and survive it? When I asked her whether she felt angry that this had happened just as she was finally realising her career dreams, she looked at me in bewilderment and said that it was the opposite; she was thankful she had had this experience just before her diagnosis, because it reminded her how great life was and gave her the strength to fight harder.

Even after being told she likely had just months left to live, Yosra decided to put on a photography exhibition in an art studio in London, featuring pictures of Beyoncé that she had taken during the tour. Using the hashtag #NeverForgettoSayThankYou, she posted photos and videos to her social media describing her journey in an effort to help others with cancer. Her posts became so popular they sparked conversations about the resources and social support available to young people battling deadly diseases. News articles were written about how Yosra's fearlessness and faith was inspiring others to tell their own stories of fighting cancer. Beyoncé herself got involved, wearing a T-shirt with 'Never Forget to Say Thank You' out in public and talking openly about Yosra's condition to the press.

One night, as I was out with friends celebrating my 34th

birthday in Cairo, Yosra's brother called to tell me she had taken a bad turn and it was near the end. It was the call I had been dreading since finding out about her diagnosis. I flew to London that night and went straight to the hospice, where she was barely able to get up or even recognise me. Her final days were excruciating, and as she slipped away her body failed her in the cruellest of ways. She died, 16 months after being diagnosed, in London, surrounded by her closest friends and family. Her last words were, 'Is that you, Shusha?' as I held her hand. I kept holding until it turned limp and heavy.

It's hard to recall exactly what happened next, perhaps because my mind had become so adept at burying these painful moments. But I remember putting my head down on the bed next to her body and closing my eyes, thinking that when I next opened them, I would be living in a world where Yosra no longer existed. I had never known that world before, and I didn't want to.

My best friend was gone, but I wasn't ready to lose her. And as much as everyone told me to be thankful for the time we had together, all I felt was anger for the future we had lost.

———

I had returned to Cairo two days after Yosra's death, dogged by a dull sadness. I expected the feeling would ease with time; that's what everyone told me. But as the months passed, I found that there were days when, without reason or warning, it felt as though she had died all over again.

It was hard to explain, even to my boyfriend, who was doing his best to lift my spirits. He too was struggling to stay hopeful, given the situation in Egypt and my colleagues' continuing detention. Many of his activist friends were being arrested or threatened; some had decided to leave Egypt and continue their advocacy from abroad, where at least they had the freedom to talk openly about el-Sisi's crackdown.

Then, all of a sudden, in August 2015, more than a year and a half after my colleagues' arrest, we finally got some good news about their case. The Court of Appeals had agreed to a retrial.

The trial proceeded in the ludicrous manner typical of the Egyptian court system. Lawyers shouted and cursed at each other, and the judge often napped during testimonies. Irrelevant and bizarre videos were shown by the prosecution to try to back up their baseless claim that the journalists were foreign agents trying to bring down the Egyptian government. My boyfriend and I went to every trial day, watching with a mixture of fear for our colleagues and embarrassment at the utter chaos of the proceedings. Mohamed Fahmy hired international human rights lawyer Amal Clooney, who worked on his case and even flew to Cairo and sat with us in the courtroom as the verdict was handed down. But our advocacy and Amal Clooney's presence weren't enough. Mohamed and the others were re-sentenced, this time to three years in prison.

Once again, the world reacted in horror. The Committee to Protect Journalists decried the trial as a sham and designated Egypt one of the riskiest places in the world to be a journalist.

We knew from government officials that el-Sisi was feeling the public pressure; he had tried to distance himself from the verdict, claiming that he had no say over the judicial process. By now, even the White House had weighed in on behalf of the condemned journalists. But the courtroom felt like a different world, one where establishment judges could take their revenge on 'disruptors' with impunity.

We had to keep exerting pressure on the president. I suspected that he was growing tired of the criticism regarding the Al Jazeera detentions. Every time he was written about in the press or held a news conference about anything, the case would be mentioned. There were demonstrations outside Egyptian embassies all over the world, where banners criticising the president and comparing him to Mubarak were waved. He needed a way to get rid of this case, but without losing face or being seen to intervene in the legal process.

His opportunity came just a month after the Appeals verdict, on Eid al-Adha, a Muslim holiday when the president tradition-ally issues pardons. Years had passed since the journalists had been apprehended, and now the news came in a simple tweet from the spokesperson of the foreign ministry: 'President el-Sisi just issued a Presidential pardon releasing 100 Egyptian activists including Al Jazeera reporter Mohamed Fahmy and others.'

The news travelled fast and was met by tears of relief from the men's families. Their ordeal was over just as quickly as it had started. President el-Sisi was able to save face: he was a dictator, but a benevolent one. I spoke to Mohamed Fahmy the day after his release and visited him shortly afterwards. For Mohamed, there was little doubt the decision was a result of the coordinated campaign launched against the regime and President el-Sisi in particular. It was a moment of joy and relief, perhaps the first time I had felt either for the country since the day Mubarak was ousted. Despite the fact there were thousands of others still wrongfully imprisoned in Egypt, it was also a moment of hope. I had felt the power of collective and determined action, and enjoyed the challenge of figuring out how to exert maximum pressure on the regime. I was not just reporting the details of a story, but lobbying and strategising to change its outcome. Our work had made a difference. Had it not been for this unrelenting advocacy of so many people, Mohamed and the others could have spent many more years behind bars.

———

The intense atmosphere in Egypt and the dramatic events we were witnessing had brought my boyfriend and me closer. We spent long nights in cafes in Zamalek, drinking fresh juice and smoking water pipes as we discussed the future of Egypt and el-Sisi's regime. If only he could be that vocal and eloquent about where our relationship was headed, I thought. Marriage seemed like a natural next step; we were both in our mid-30s and had been together a few years. But he never discussed it, so despite our friends and families prodding, I didn't bring it up. My boyfriend was not the traditional type. He had rebelled against society's expectations in every way he could, and given that his own parents and many of his other family members were divorced, he had made it clear he was not a fan of marriage. Unlike him, I wanted to get married, but maybe I had inherited my parents' non-confrontational technique of staying quiet in these moments. Still, he understood that the community around us, including his own family, was growing impatient.

Feeling the need to take a break from Egypt and work, we

decided to go on holiday to Barcelona as a couple. He seemed very excited about the trip, which I thought was another way to try to cheer me up — despite how much time had passed, I was still consumed with grief and confusion over Yosra's death. As soon as we got to our hotel, he made a plan to take me to the Tibidabo amusement park, beautifully situated on the top of a mountain on the outskirts of the city. The main attraction was a large Ferris wheel, and he insisted that we take a ride in one of its brightly coloured carriages.

As soon as we sat down, he put his arms around me and started to whisper in my ear how much he loved me. I was surprised — he rarely expressed his emotions like that or said the words 'I love you' — and for a moment I even wondered if the altitude was getting to him. Then, suddenly, as we sat overlooking the city, he took a little box out of his pocket and asked me to be his wife. He promised to love and cherish me, talked about the adventures we would have and about growing old together.

He had said all the things that I had dreamed a man would one day say to me. I looked into his big round eyes and, as I unhesitatingly said yes, I saw his joy and genuine relief. My heart still felt heavy from losing Yosra, and we were still going through so much disappointment in Egypt, but this moment felt like a sweet respite. Finally, some good news amid the despair.

We got off the Ferris wheel and celebrated in the park, sitting on a wooden bench eating mini hotdogs and drinking Prosecco from plastic cups as we planned out our future together. We discussed leaving Egypt, and I imagined myself starting again in a new country as a wife, and hopefully a mother, too, away from protests and wars. I also, strangely, felt a strong sense of relief. No matter how much professional success I enjoyed, I was acutely aware that I was considered to be 'behind' in my personal life. So many of the friends I had grown up with were already married with children. Both my siblings had kids; my sister's eldest son was almost ten years old. My parents were very supportive of my choices, but even they were growing bored of their friends asking them why I wasn't married. The community I grew up in had gone from being proud to regarding me with an attitude of passive disapproval, as though I had taken things too far. Professional success was all very well; but working, it seemed, was just what women did while waiting for a husband.

Perhaps a part of me thought this new, more normal life would give me the fulfilment I was craving and had not yet found through my work. I wished so much that I could call up Yosra and tell her that I was engaged. She would have been so happy for us.

12.

Big Day

I woke up on my wedding day earlier, and more irritated, than usual. The sun's light was shooting into the room, striking my face and exposing strands of dust on the dark parquet floor. On the street below, a vendor's shouts competed with the scattered beeps of a thousand cars and screaming children waiting for school doors to open.

Cairo inflicts a testing blend of heavy air and incessant noise on its residents. Eventually, you grow to love the imposition. But every now and again, it's suffocating.

I noticed my fiancé's light-blue pyjamas lying carelessly next to me on the bed. Taking in his smell, I folded them loosely, the same way I always did when he abandoned one set of clothes for another.

It was strange that he'd left before I'd woken up, especially given the significance of the day. I reached for my phone and saw a message from him: 'I'm at the protest, be home soon,' it read. It was so casual I thought nothing of it.

I resisted the urge to fall into my reporter routine — scrolling through Twitter, calling Leila to see what she'd heard, checking Twitter again. Protests against President el-Sisi were scarce since it had become so dangerous for demonstrators to be out on the streets. The brief flash of freedom we had felt after the uprising was now well and truly gone.

My fiancé and I were due to sign our papers at the registry office that afternoon, exactly one year after the proposal. The countdown would then begin to our wedding party a few weeks later — we had invited 400 guests to celebrate with us on the French Riviera. Afterwards, our plan was to move to New York, where my fiancé had a job lined up at a newly launched American non-profit news organisation. I wasn't sure what I wanted to do in New York. I'd briefly taken the job with Sky News, setting up their Cairo bureau, but it had only exacerbated my frustration with journalism. Television news was becoming increasingly superficial, placing the reporter at the centre of the story. No longer was our role guiding and narrating reports; we needed to show the audience that we were right there on the front lines, even if dramatically putting ourselves in danger didn't actually further our understanding of what was going on. The riskier we made it look, the more the bosses loved it and the more awards we won. Travelling constantly all over the region, barely spending more than a week at a time in one place — including Cairo — yanked from one story to another, I had found myself unable to physically recover from, let alone emotionally digest, what I was seeing.

Despite the patience of my editors, and in particular Sky's foreign editor, Dan Williams, it had become clear that I was burning out. Just like after the Gaza War, I quickly lost motivation for the work and felt numb most of the time. The familiar feeling of emptiness and guilt returned: I was doing nothing to change the lives of the people I reported on. Ever since I had taken a break from journalism and campaigned on behalf of my AJE colleagues, reporting had felt less and less satisfying. When the so-called Islamic State group began destroying ancient monuments and temples in the Syrian city of Palmyra, Sky News had put me on television talking about the ruined artefacts for days at a time. I remember questioning Dan every time he assigned me to the story, asking, 'What's the point of me commenting on this?'

'These are pieces of history that are being erased — it's newsworthy!' he would answer, astounded that I was arguing with him. He was right. The looting and destruction of an ancient city by a group of terrorists was a significant story and a legitimate one. But my interest was no longer in telling people about the bad things going on in the world. Even when I was interviewing Syrian refugees, telling their harrowing stories of escaping Islamic State fighters and getting on makeshift boats to flee to Europe, that feeling of uselessness and powerlessness returned. Rather, my interest was in trying to do something to stop these injustices from happening. If there was no such instruction, no clear message in the report, I simply didn't see the value in what I was doing. That's why, when my fiancé had said he wanted to move to New York after the wedding, I had jumped at the opportunity, and resigned from Sky News.

I had also started looking into the work of Amnesty

International and Human Rights Watch, the two largest global human rights organisations. A contact at Amnesty put me in touch with one of the senior directors, who was recruiting for a head of their office at the United Nations in New York. Despite my lack of human rights experience, they agreed to interview me remotely from London via Zoom, but the only day they could make it was the morning before we were due at the registry office. I was intrigued by the role and excited at the possibility of working as an advocate, but I was also hesitant to make such a drastic career change; journalism was all I knew. The almost cult-like nature of the media industry has a way of making you feel like you are part of a privileged, elite club, and that there is nothing half as fun or worthy waiting if you leave. Also, I wasn't sure the timing would work, because Amnesty needed someone to start right away, and I had the wedding party and moving to deal with.

I hadn't prepared for the interview much beyond quickly scrolling through Amnesty's website the night before, as I sat on the plane back from my bachelorette party in Dubai. I knew I should get out of bed and do some reading up on Amnesty's campaigns, but this was my Big Day and I didn't feel like doing any work.

I was wrestling with these thoughts when I heard the front door slam. Seconds later, my fiancé appeared, standing by the bedroom door. But my wide smile was met by a frown.

'Come to the living room,' he said. 'We need to talk.'

We sat down on the sofa facing each other; I had to push aside a pile of bridal magazines to make space. A few of the heavier ones dropped to the floor, opening to reveal pages whose corners I had turned down as I researched my wedding. I smiled at how ridiculously chunky they were — when had I become a girl who was obsessed with table centrepieces and colour themes? We had originally imagined a small wedding, but somewhere along the way the wedding industry — with its party planners and florists — had taken a hold of me, and all I wanted to do with my free time was look at venues on Instagram and play around with my Pinterest theme board.

I placed the magazines neatly back on the table in front of us and leaned into the sofa.

'How are the protests looking outside? Nasty, huh?' I asked, placing my feet on his lap.

Seconds passed, and he still wasn't answering me. Instead, he was staring at the floor as if deep in thought. I started talking over his silence, excitedly catching him up on my bachelorette party and how some of my friends had surprised me by travelling all the way from London. I was about to ask him what he thought I should do to prepare for the Amnesty interview, when he looked up at me with a face full of confusion, or perhaps fear. I was startled: I'd seen his face after a bomb blast, after our friends were arrested by the police, after he had lost a loved one. But I'd never seen him look like he looked now.

'My mum and dad are very angry, Sherine,' he told me, as if our parents arguing was something new. His parents were Muslim, and although our religious differences had never been an issue for us, ever since we had announced our engagement, a war had been brewing between our parents. Each side believed that they would be making the larger sacrifices to make the marriage work. The latest fight was about wedding invitations.

I apologised for being absent the last couple of days and for my family's meddling — admitting that this time my parents were the guilty party. I told him I would figure it out, suggesting various solutions to try to calm the situation. Compromises that we could each take back to our parents. I was good at this. I could fix it.

Suddenly, in mid-flow, he stopped speaking and covered his face with his hands. I hoped that he was quietly working out a solution. But when his hands fell, he locked me in a stare so intense that my mind emptied.

'I'm sorry. I can't do this,' he said. 'I don't think I love you *enough.*'

The words fell out of his mouth so effortlessly and precisely that it felt like everything he had ever said to me in the past had been forced, and now he was finally telling me the truth.

He went on, but I couldn't hear what he was saying because a chattering voice in my head got so loud it took over, distracting me from the reality of what I was hearing — *What am I going to do with all the pashminas I have commissioned embroidered with our wedding date? Maybe we can get the deposit back from the photographer if we explain what's happened? I can't believe I whitened my teeth for no reason.*

But the more he spoke, the heavier my limbs became, until I could hardly move. I knew what he was saying was serious, and yet I couldn't absorb the full gravity of it. He was talking quickly and looking straight into my eyes as tears streamed down his face. He admitted that the latest fight between our parents had given him a way out, an excuse to call off the wedding. I realised that during all these years, and all the hard times we had experienced together, I had never seen him cry.

It was happening so fast. I kept thinking, *Why now? Why wait until today to tell me?* The question seemed so present, so reasonable and necessary; and yet I couldn't say a word.

My journalist brain, trained to keep asking and digging and analysing, relented. All my questions were useless, too late.

The doorbell rang, and for a moment he looked relieved.

'I texted Leila to come over,' he explained.

He knew he was going to do this, I thought. *If he contacted Leila beforehand, it means he had a plan. How long has he known?* I wondered silently as the anger began to set in.

He opened the door, and Leila walked straight in, standing between us, moving her eyes from his face to mine. I could tell immediately that she didn't know what was going on. She was full of questions: What had happened? Why was he crying? Why weren't we dressed for the registry office? But he had no answers, not even for her. Instead, he walked around us, packing up his things as if we were ghosts, avoiding the stacks of bridal magazines and my Vera Wang wedding dress hanging in the corner of the room, the long lace veil peering out of its huge cream-coloured cover.

'Take care of her,' he said to Leila so quietly it was almost a whisper, closing the door behind him.

Another statement without explanation. Another broken promise. *I thought taking care of me was meant to be his job — isn't that what he promised he would do when he proposed?*

Leila sat down next to me on the sofa, staring at the door as if waiting for it to tell her what had happened in this room in the last hour that could have caused all this destruction. She wrapped her arms so tightly around my torso that it felt like it wasn't just for comfort; she was restraining me. As if she was afraid of what I would do if she let go.

'Are you going to be okay for a few minutes alone?' Leila asked, watching me fiddle with my engagement ring, twisting it from the back with my thumb. 'I'm going to go and get your parents. I'll be right back.'

As the door shut, my muscles released and I fell to the floor like I'd been shot. I could feel my heart pounding, and pressed the palm of my hand against my chest, as if trying to stop a catastrophic bleed. The tears fell uncontrollably. I exhaled hard, over and over again, trying to force all the air out of my body. But my chest wouldn't cooperate; it kept trying to draw oxygen back in. Trying to save a life I didn't want anymore. Now that I was alone in the apartment, it was finally sinking in. He wasn't coming back, and all I could think about was how much I already missed him.

I knew fairy tales weren't real. Yet somehow, over the four years of the relationship, I had come to believe in ours. Everyone thought we were in love, and I had let myself believe that, too. I had silenced the voice in my head telling me that he never quite seemed sure, that perhaps it wasn't marriage he was hesitant about, it was me. I had believed that a Christian woman and a Muslim man could be together in the new Egypt. I had believed the country was changing for the better, and that I had played a small role in that. I had believed that perhaps I could be both an activist and a journalist, and that a woman could have a successful career and a meaningful personal life.

Now all those beliefs were crumbling, exposed as silly aspirations born of a privileged, naïve view of the world. I sat on the floor and cried, taking in the reality that I now had no husband, no job, and nowhere to live.

I'd spent my career witnessing all kinds of catastrophes, and I knew that life could be unpredictable, but I'd had no idea that the future I'd planned could be taken away without warning not just by a political crisis, a war, or a natural disaster, but by an emotional cataclysm over which I had zero control. I didn't know where my former fiancé had gone, or what I was going to do to put my life back together.

―――――

By the time Leila came back an hour later, I had got up, washed my face, and filled three large garbage bags with my belongings. My mother was standing in the doorway behind her, as if waiting for my instruction to come in. She looked pale, and a large blue vein was protruding from the centre of her forehead.

'What are you doing, Sherine?' she asked softly.

'Help me pack,' I barked, throwing the roll of plastic garbage bags at Leila.

'Pack what?' Leila asked.

'Anything that's mine, looks like it could be mine, or that you think I would like. If in doubt, pack it,' I demanded.

They both looked at me blankly. There was probably much more they wanted to say, to tell me to take my time, that I didn't have to do this now. But they knew better. I had made my mind up — I was leaving.

'Wasn't that the gift you got him for his birthday?' Leila asked, watching me stuff the Apple TV box and its wires into a bag.

'You're right,' I said. 'Then I'll only take the remote.'

While normal packing is about being tidy and efficient,

revenge packing is about removing every trace of yourself, except the things that could cause him pain or annoyance.

Two hours and 13 garbage bags later, we were done. I went back into the bedroom, where his pyjamas were still folded on top of the unmade bed. So much had happened since this morning, and yet everything looked exactly the same. I stared at the wardrobe leaning against the wall, remembering the time we stayed up all night attempting to put it together and vowing never to buy anything from IKEA again.

I took my engagement ring off and placed it on his bedside table, along with the wedding bands we were meant to have worn that afternoon. Then I took the key to the apartment off my key chain and left it next to the rings. This was no longer my home.

We dragged the bags to the elevator, and as I closed the front door, I paused, remembering all the times I had come back from reporting trips, excitedly turning the key in the lock and seeing him sitting on the sofa waiting for me with his feet up on the table and a goofy smile. It was the first time since leaving Number 29 that I had actually felt like I had a home.

I turned away from the door and headed for the elevator. I knew I would never go back to that apartment again.

My parents and I took the next flight to London, which departed at midnight Cairo time and arrived in the early hours of the following morning. I cried the whole journey back, burying my face in my mother's chest like a child while I avoided people's stares. She tried to ask me what had happened at the apartment, but I had no energy to recount the story, nor had I any answers. I just kept telling her it was over, that he had left me. My father barely said a word the entire time, but every so often he would take my hand and squeeze it to let me know he was there for me. He called my brother and sister and told them what had happened. They had both recently moved to Dubai with their families, but they immediately booked flights to London, leaving their kids and work in a panic. It felt like someone had died.

'It's the first time we'll all be at Number 29 together since you left London,' my mother told me, 'and Leila said she'll also come.' She was trying to sound upbeat.

As soon as we arrived at Number 29, I went to my bedroom and locked the door, relieved to be within safe walls and among familiar smells. Some of Yosra's clothes were still hanging in my wardrobe: I had kept her oversized T-shirts and even a pair of her sneakers. I looked at them, and wished fervently that she could be with me now.

It was peaceful at Number 29, and I slept deeply there, aided by a cocktail of antidepressants that my mother got from a friend of hers. Unlike the previous times I had sought refuge at my childhood home, now I was under no time pressure. There was no job to go back to, and I had no trips planned. I could stay here, like this, for ever if I wanted to. There was nobody to disappoint, no duty to be fulfilled. I had been so busy for the preceding weeks and months that even a few hours of idleness had felt like a catastrophic waste of time. Now, nothing was expected of me.

The next morning, just as the sun was rising, I walked out of the front door of Number 29 still wearing my pyjamas. I didn't know where I was going or what I wanted to do. I had taken more antidepressants along with sleeping pills and could barely feel my legs moving. I crossed the road next to the house and stood dazed in the middle of the dual carriageway. My father must have heard the front door closing, because seconds later he was running after me in bare feet and a nightrobe. He ran into the road and grabbed my arm, pulling me to the pavement. My mother came running towards us, holding up the hem of her long silk nightgown. We sat on the hard cement for a few minutes to catch our breath, before my father led us silently back inside the house.

I don't know what I was trying to do that day. I don't believe I really wanted to get run over; I hope I would have moved out of the way if I had seen a car coming. But I can't be sure. As we sat in the living room, I kept my head down, avoiding Jesus' blue eyes on the mantle, or Mary's open arms on the walls. I didn't want their judgement today. I didn't want to be reminded of how self-ish I was for putting my family through this pain, or how grateful I ought to be for all that I still had.

My mother made us breakfast, and eventually my father spoke.

'You will recover from this,' he said, as though choking on the words, 'and you will have a great life. I know this because you have not wronged anyone. *You* did nothing wrong, and God protects the good. You'll see.'

I hugged him and said I was sorry, over and over again. After a while, my mother switched the television on, and we sat there on our large green leather sofa, the same way we did when I was a child. If Yosra had been there, I thought, she would have made us all milky tea.

After breakfast, I went upstairs and managed a shower. I changed into fresh clothes that I found in my wardrobe from when I was a teenager. I had left the garbage bags full of my belongings, including my clothes, at my parents' house in Cairo.

Feeling a little better, I decided it was time to check my phone. I sifted through all the messages from concerned friends and scrolled down until I found what I was looking for. It was an email from Katherine Ofori, assistant to the senior director at Amnesty International.

The email said that my interview had been cancelled after I had failed to show up. I wrote back saying that I'd had an emergency, apologising profusely and asking for another chance, informing her that I was now in London and could meet in person.

I could have tried to get my position back at Sky News: Dan would have been sympathetic, and they hadn't replaced me yet. But suddenly I was determined to get the Amnesty job. It was as if when nothing was expected of me, when all was lost and I could start again, I knew exactly what I needed to do. Away from Egypt, my fiancé, and everyone's expectations, my hesitation over joining Amnesty dissipated. Leaving journalism was no longer the hard choice but the only one that made any sense. There were so many unknowns in that moment, but what I was sure about was that I wanted to be a human rights advocate.

Katherine Ofori replied to my email ten minutes later, informing me that the panel could convene to interview me but it had to be that afternoon. They could forgive my no-show, and it was a good opportunity to meet in person. I confirmed the details with her just as my brother and sister arrived at Number 29, looking tired and worried.

I ran down the stairs and hugged them both, thanking them for coming all the way so quickly. My brother held me extra tight. 'I could kill him for doing this,' he whispered in my ear.

My sister's reaction was to go into full-on organisation mode. 'Okay, so there's a lot to do. Where shall we start?' she said, referring to undoing the wedding party plans. She was already holding her laptop under her arm and heading towards the kitchen table, mumbling something about the gift registry.

'Actually, I have a job interview in a few hours,' I replied, watching them turn all at once and look at me in amazement. This was not what they had been expecting me to say.

'But first, we need to go to Zara. I have no clothes!' I continued, looking down at the ancient jeans I'd pulled out of my cupboard and dressed myself in.

I ran back up the stairs to get my shoes while the four of them stood there silently, wondering if I had lost my mind.

13.

The House Where
the World Meets

New York is the perfect city for the broken-hearted. After I got the Amnesty job, I moved there as soon as I could, discovering that at every party I went to there were new and interesting people to meet, which in turn led to invitations to gallery openings, film screenings, the launch of a new bar. Everyone I encountered seemed to be moving house or starting a new job. Reinvention is normal in New York, part of the American model of growth and success. Here, my radical change in personal and professional circumstances was greeted with a congratulatory toast, and not the sad 'this too shall pass' reactions I was getting in London. I met people who had gone from being Wall Street bankers to yoga teachers overnight, and, on one occasion, a successful lawyer who decided to quit and become a 'death doula' — quite literally a coach for people who are dying. Change wasn't feared here, it was encouraged.

Coincidentally, Ayman had also moved to New York several months before me, taking up a new role at MSNBC as a correspondent and occasional host. Being at the network's headquarters gave him an opportunity to show that he could transition from reporting on the ground to anchoring live shows in the studio. His coverage in Gaza and Egypt had made clear that it was not just his reporting, but the analysis and commentary he offered around it, that made him stand out as a journalist. He had another motivation for leaving Egypt, too: his girlfriend at the time, a Tunisian supermodel called Kenza Fourati, lived in New York, and things were getting more serious between them. I met Kenza when I first arrived in New York, at a coffee shop in Greenwich Village, standing at the counter chatting happily with the barista. Her hair was in a loose ponytail and she was wearing blue jeans that stopped just above her elegant ankles, topped by a loose white T-shirt tucked in at the front. I was taken aback by this beautiful creature with a huge smile and endless limbs, but she ran over and hugged me as if we were best friends who hadn't seen each other for years. Her warmth and ease reminded me of Yosra, and I felt an instant connection to her. She and Ayman were married that summer, and they bought an apartment in Brooklyn overlooking the East River.

I found a nearby place to rent and, a few months later, my friend Leila moved in with me. She too needed a break from journalism and had accepted a fellowship at the Council on Foreign Relations, based in Midtown Manhattan. Somehow, unplanned, I found myself surrounded by my closest friends, each one of them determined to do everything possible to help me forget about my sadness — from taking me away for weekends upstate, to buying me passes for intense workout classes.

I embraced the distractions, which included my new job. At first, just like in journalism, I had no idea what I was doing. I was a rookie again. Amnesty's office was in a building housing dozens of other non-governmental organisations. Just across the road was the UN headquarters, where I spent most of my time. I had heard a tour guide once describe the building as 'the house where the world meets'. But nothing could have prepared me for the gigantic maze of conference rooms, chambers, offices, cafeterias, prayer areas, gift shops, private floors, and scattered exhibitions in abandoned corners. I kept getting lost, but no matter how desperate I was, I refused to ask for help. I was head of the UN office for the largest human rights organisation in the world, in charge of nine senior advocates — there was no way I was going to ask for directions to the restrooms. My colleagues at Amnesty had warned me before coming out how difficult it was to 'get in the room' where decisions were being made. I couldn't even find the room.

The UN is known for all the different languages spoken during meetings, with 193 member states from around the world represented. But what is less known is that the UN has its own unofficial language spoken only by those who work with or at the UN. This is a series of terms and acronyms that everyone drops so frequently and thoughtlessly that it becomes impossible to stop and ask what they are referring to. To some extent, all big organisations end up using jargon, but the UN takes this to an absurd level. In my first week, I sat through entire meetings in which I understood absolutely nothing, not even what the meeting was about. Even when I scheduled meetings myself to talk about our advocacy strategy on refugees or a new Amnesty report coming out, it was impossible to keep up. 'Why don't you seek bilats with *wee-yog*? Friendlies that signed the MOU,' was a colleague's advice to me at one such meeting. I looked around me; everyone else was nodding. I felt like a con man who has duped everyone around him into thinking he's an expert, and is now praying nobody finds out. All I could do to mask my total ignorance was agree: 'Sounds good,' I said more than once, with no idea what I was agreeing to. In that case, unbeknown to me, I had committed to setting up individual, private meetings for Amnesty with states known as WEOG, the Western European and Other States Group, including Western Asia. The UN divides member states into five regional groups, in order to distribute membership quotas and leadership positions. Many of those in the WEOG had signed a memorandum of understanding (or MOU), so would likely be sympathetic to our cause. Understanding was easy, but only once you knew the lingo.

It was not just the new words or acronyms that caught me out. Even seemingly ordinary phrases take on different meanings in a UN context. If you want to say that something is important but you have no plan for how to get it done, you start talking about 'mainstreaming' it. This sounds like a great thing to do, to make sure whatever you are prioritising is embedded throughout different UN departments, but nobody ever really knows how to 'mainstream' when we are talking about a huge organisation like the UN. Like most jargon, it also makes you sound smart to outsiders, while actually saying very basic things.

When the senior director, Tawanda, sent an email asking me what our 'UNGA plans' were, I quickly had to google 'UNGA' to make sure I knew what he was talking about. It was, of course, the UN General Assembly. An event takes place at UN headquarters in New York every year in mid-September to mark the opening of the new session of the General Assembly. All 193 leaders of the countries represented at the UN descend on New York to give speeches during what is known as High-Level Week, or, more informally, Leaders' Week. With every influential public figure in the world attending UNGA, the UN building becomes a hotbed for political sightings. In a single afternoon, you can see anyone from Angelina Jolie to the Chinese premier hurry by as they head to meetings. Even the most seasoned diplomats can't help but enjoy the people-watching.

For Amnesty, it's an opportunity for our secretary-general to network among decision-makers and speak at prestigious side events. The world's media camps outside the UN building, reporting on what is being said by the leaders inside. The most significant meetings happen behind closed doors, as world leaders use the opportunity of the gathering to negotiate with their counterparts in person. My job was to make sure our secretary-general was invited to as many meetings as possible, in order to have opportunities to give our perspective on world events and make recommendations directly to policymakers.

My first ever high-level meeting during UNGA was with the leader of a medium-sized, influential country. It was a private briefing with a few selected heads of non-governmental organisations (NGOs), including Amnesty International. After various security checks, the secretary-general of Amnesty and I were led into a large conference room with an oversized oval table in the centre surrounded by grey fabric chairs.

Along the perimeter of the room was a second row of less comfortable-looking chairs, with their backs against the eggshell-coloured walls. The Amnesty secretary-general was instructed to sit down at the table, and I was directed to the fold-up chair behind him. The place setting consisted of a small rectangular box with a screen reading 'Amnesty International' at the front of it. At one end of the box was a thin black microphone, and at the other a long wire leading to a small, curved, plastic earshell. There were also various buttons sunk into the table. The room wasn't that big, and there were only around 20 people — *why would anyone need a microphone?* I thought. My counterpart from Human Rights Watch saw me staring at the box and kindly whispered, 'It's for translation. You speak into the microphone and the translators will feed back what you're saying into that plastic earshell in whatever your preferred language is.'

Suddenly, I felt myself getting uncomfortably hot, despite the blasting air conditioner. I had interviewed heads of state before; I hadn't anticipated getting nervous in a meeting where I wasn't even expected to speak. But I was intimidated by this foreign environment, where everyone seemed to know the rules but me. I could usually fake knowledge about a topic with confidence, but this room was full of things that instantly exposed me as a novice.

Although the diplomats who organised the meeting had told me it would be 'informal', we had spent days beforehand agreeing on everything from the seating plan to the order of questions and how long each representative would have to speak. I quickly learned that there is no such thing as informal at the UN. The bar starts at formal and goes upwards until you reach the level of a fully choreographed opera. There are rules for how you address the different levels of diplomats, how you thank people, how you start your speech, what you even call your speech (it's an 'intervention'). Rules I had had no idea existed.

The leader walked in, surrounded by four other people — two in black suits and what looked like bulletproof vests under their shirts, and another two armed with thick black folders. They all looked very important and in a great hurry. Despite the stuffy environment, I was struck by how down to earth the leader was, walking around the table greeting every person with a handshake, even the assistants. Even me. He was being followed by a photographer snapping the quick interactions, stepping on everyone's toes apologetically as he tried to keep up.

The leader sat down and said a few words about the valued work of NGOs, a speech I would hear repeated many times by many leaders from different countries. Another rule: always thank everyone for taking the meeting and tell them how important they are as soon as you sit down, no matter how 'informal' the meeting is or who it's with. It struck me how emphatically he spoke about NGO presence at the UN, how our job was to hold leaders like him accountable and also to bring a human rights perspective to every issue. I saw the other representatives smiling and nodding their heads. I wondered why they all looked so happy at having their jobs explained to them. This slightly absurd talk went on for several minutes, before he opened up the conversation, promising a 'frank' discussion among friends.

The NGO representatives sat up, shuffling their notes

anxiously; they each had only five minutes to speak. I had discussed with my colleagues at Amnesty which topics we would bring up, and coordinated with some of the other organisations to make sure as many issues as possible would be covered. It was a challenge to decide which situations we could raise and which we simply did not have time for. My decisions were based on which issues this leader had the power to do something about, rather than the topics we should mention out of moral duty. It was hard to balance pragmatism and principle, and not everyone agreed on how that balance should tip. For me in that moment, it was about leaving the room having achieved something for the people we were trying to help; a promise to look into a certain case or use their leverage to press on human rights abuses. Given that was the goal, I wasn't going to waste my time with asks that I knew that leader would not have the power to make happen.

As we went around the table, I became increasingly frustrated at the NGO representatives making their interventions. Much time was spent saying thank you for the meeting and even, in some cases, recounting stories of past meetings with the leader. What a tragic waste of seconds, I thought. I understood the need for formalities and maintaining a good relationship, but was it really necessary to thank them quite so much simply for taking one hour out of their schedule to meet? But this habit of wasting time with empty words is so expected at the UN that to veer from it and say anything pertinent right at the start is considered abrupt and rude. It occurred to me how awkward the meeting was, each interaction proceeding like a date that's going badly, with both parties treading on eggshells. Several minutes would pass without anyone making a single point of any substance.

When it was time for my boss, the head of Amnesty International, to speak, I felt my heart racing just like it had before I went live on television. This time, though, it wasn't because I was worried about messing up or falling off a chair during an interview, but because I felt an awesome sense of responsibility. We had just a few minutes in front of a man who had the power to end people's suffering. I recognised what an incredible platform we had and what messing it up would mean. *I am a tree*, I kept telling myself, breathing deeply.

My boss thanked the leader and then began talking about the situation in Egypt, just as we had agreed. President el-Sisi was continuing with his campaign of unlawful killings, enforced disappearances, and torture. Certain UN member states had just authorised the sale of military equipment to Cairo worth over six billion dollars — arms that el-Sisi would turn on his own people if they protested against him — and now we were calling on those states to halt the sales. As a financial supporter of Egypt, we knew this leader could pressure President el-Sisi into slowing his crackdown. My boss spoke of the responsibility the leader had to make sure any deals with Egypt were not aiding tyranny. He also mentioned the case of Egyptian blogger Alaa Abd el-Fattah, an activist and friend who had been arrested and jailed several times since the uprising in 2011, simply for protesting. After his latest arrest, a UN working group had issued a statement calling for his release, so it was a good time to bring up his case.

Just as my boss was running out of time, made clear by the leader's aide waving her arms at me from across the room, he quickly mentioned the refugee crisis as a result of the war in Syria, and the need to take in those fleeing the violence.

As my boss finished, I sat up, ready to write down every word the leader was about to say, to report it back to our teams in confidence.

'On arms sales to Egypt ... well, no.' The reply was so blunt that I dropped my pen on the floor in surprise.

He explained that the question of arms sales was deeper than my boss had presented, that countries needed to make sure Egypt was well armed because it was fighting an insurgency in the Sinai Peninsula against terrorists, including from the Islamic State group. He repeated many of the justifications President el-Sisi offered in his speeches. As long as Egypt was dealing with this problem, it would continue to receive military support.

'Even if those weapons are also being used against civilians, including in the Sinai?' asked my boss, bravely breaking with protocol to ask a follow-up question. The leader knew he could not answer that question; to admit to knowing the weapons were being used illegally would make his country complicit. In a condescending tone he replied, 'It's complicated.'

He quickly moved on, not addressing the case of my friend Alaa. I hoped at least that one of the leader's advisors had written down Alaa's name somewhere. On Syria, there was lots of concern and shaking of his head and sighing. But again, ultimately, he explained the limits of what his country could do to absorb another's population. He tipped his head to the side and shrugged his shoulders, and with that we moved on to the next person's five minutes.

I walked out of the meeting feeling deflated. I hadn't been expecting to change his mind there and then, but his easy dismissal of our concerns made me feel as useless as handing chocolate bars out to starving kids in a Cairo slum had. We had an audience with a world leader, but what power did NGOs like mine really have? I wondered if I had chosen the wrong issues to present; perhaps I had aimed too high by raising Egypt and Syria.

The question weighed me down as I made my way through the security checks and barriers to the next meeting. I was headed to the General Assembly building for the opening ceremony. I found my way to the upper balcony of the hall, which was already packed with my colleagues and counterparts from other NGOs. Despite the praise we got from leaders for being a force for good at the UN, we were, at best, treated like guests in the building. Although we were fully vetted and accredited, we had to use the 'tourist' entrance, waiting in long security lines every day. Once inside, we were barred from certain floors and meeting rooms, and given the nosebleed seats at important events.

Still, I was glad to be there and excited about hearing the UN high commissioner for human rights, Zeid bin Ra'ad bin Zeid al-Hussein, give an address about Syrian refugees. That year, heads of state were congratulating themselves for finally signing the New York Declaration for Refugees and Migrants, an agreement that was meant to show global political solidarity for protecting the vulnerable. In reality, it was a lot of nice words on paper that would do nothing to actually help the immense and growing needs of displaced people. The leaders had successfully ticked the humanitarian box at the summit without having to make a single commitment to take in refugees, or change policy. I thought back to what I had said in my interview with Amnesty a few months before, that we should be advocating for these refugees to have their basic rights respected by their host countries. The declaration seemed to acknowledge the gravity of the problem, without actually doing much to solve it. I hoped the high commissioner would expose the fact that the declaration was simply a wishful act of good intention, with zero accountability.

The opening speeches were going to take a while, so I tried to get comfortable in my narrow pull-down seat, bracing myself for the pomp to come. As the high commissioner walked up to the podium, the chatter stopped, and the few people near the doors quickly hurried to their seats. This high commissioner was an anomaly at the UN, known for being outspoken and blunt, and he always drew in a crowd when he spoke. He began powerfully, doing away with the long ceremonial thanks and welcomes of others. He told the gathered leaders that the international community had been failing the Syrian people and millions of refugees. He called their suffering 'shameful' and told the diplomats in the room that they were responsible.

'You may walk away from this hall, but not from the broader judgement of "we, the people", all the world's people — not from us,' said High Commissioner al-Hussein.

It was an electrifying speech, punctuated by cheers coming from those around me in the gallery.

The leaders in their seats below looked uncomfortable, twitching and whispering to their aides. Moments before, they had been patting themselves on the back for adopting the declaration. Now, they were being called out for failing once again to come up with any binding commitments that would help the Syrian people. I watched the leader I had met with earlier frowning. He had shrugged us off that morning when we had spoken about the refugees, but now I could see him below, staring at the high commissioner with a troubled expression. At one point, he wrote something down for his aide to read, and I thought perhaps he was asking him to set up a meeting with al-Hussein, or perhaps the refugee commissioner, while he was in New York. I hoped our words of warning from that morning were in some way getting through.

It was at that moment, sitting in the hall watching all the tiny leaders below, that I realised the kind of impact I'd been hoping for when I'd walked into that meeting with the leader could only happen by individuals, who believe that change is necessary and possible, coming together and demanding it. This was the same feeling I'd had watching the protestors in Tahrir Square, passionately and fearlessly demanding their rights, knowing that it was impossible for the regime to ignore their collective, determined action.

The gallery around me exploded into applause when the high commissioner finished his speech, and we gave him a standing ovation. Our cheers were so loud they prompted the guards to motion at us to sit down. 'This isn't Madison Square Garden,' one of them shouted at us, angrily. I looked over and saw the reporters hard at work inside their glass cubicles, hurriedly writing notes. I appreciated them for making sure the high commissioner's words would be heard by people across the world, but I was thankful I was not inside that box anymore, forced to observe events neutrally rather than trying to shape them.

I was exactly where I needed to be, standing up and taking a side.

14.

Small Wins, High Stakes

I stared at the picture of the little girl wearing a dirty pink jacket and standing amid rubble. She was biting her hand, and didn't look scared so much as cold and lost. The thin black straps of her sandals were covered in dust from the debris surrounding her feet.

Beneath the photo were the words: 'How 2016 became the worst year for Syria's children.'

'What's that?' Leila asked, startling me. I still wasn't used to living with someone who wasn't my fiancé. She was hurrying around our small apartment, late for a spin class she'd signed up for the previous night after we had inhaled an entire box of Krispy Kreme doughnuts.

'It's a press release that UNICEF is working on. Someone gave me a draft,' I answered. According to them, more than 600 Syrian children had been killed that year in the war, 20 per cent more than in 2015. The figures were still estimates, which meant they were likely to be even higher by the final draft.

Leila came over and started reading over my shoulder while putting on her coat.

'Are these figures for real? That's horrific,' she said.

We sat in silence. Leila continued reading while I went through the release, highlighting the shocking statistics. Six years on from the start of the war and Syria was in full-blown humanitarian crisis. Over 300,000 people had been killed in the fighting, and millions had fled their homes. Aid agencies could not keep up, and many people in need were dying from disease and malnutrition.

'At least the UN is doing something, documenting what's going on,' Leila offered, as she grabbed her keys from the table and made her way to the door.

The argument felt depressingly familiar — in the absence of being able to change these people's situation, at least there were records of their suffering.

UNICEF and the UN's other humanitarian agencies were indeed active on the ground where they could be, providing food aid and shelter for millions of refugees. But it was the political side of the UN, the Security Council, that was failing so miserably to end the war or hold those responsible for all this suffering to account.

All the books I'd read about the UN had started with the fact that it was created after the bloodshed and destruction of World War II in order to make sure a similar tragedy never happened again. At the time, multiple treaties and declarations were signed by states, in recognition that the horror of the Holocaust should never be repeated. Yet here we were, 70 years after the creation of the UN, and hundreds of thousands had been killed in Syria in a war that was showing no signs of ending. What a colossal failure.

More specifically, the members of the Security Council who had the power to impose sanctions or send in peacekeepers, and even possibly have the Syrian president, Bashar al-Assad, face the International Criminal Court one day, were doing none of those things. Al-Assad was good friends with the Russians, who had the power to stop any action being taken at the Council by using their veto. The Russians had unashamedly used that power over and over again, blocking resolutions that would have sanctioned al-Assad and perhaps even forced him to end the war.

As I sat there in my Brooklyn apartment, overlooking the East River, I suddenly felt very detached from Syria and the people there. I was far away from the refugee camps in Lebanon and Turkey that I had spent so much time in. When I left journalism, I'd decided that I could make more of an impact from afar, by being in the place where decisions were made and not always where their consequences were being felt. It was why I had joined Amnesty — so that it would be my job to try to stop the suffering. But in that moment, looking down at the photo of the little Syrian girl, I wondered if I had expected too much from this job, and whether I was really using all the tools at my disposal to affect the situation.

It gave me something to think about on my walk to the subway that morning. We only lived one stop from Manhattan, but somehow the journey to Midtown took almost an hour. I sat down on one of the train's orange plastic chairs that looked like they should have been replaced a decade ago, praying the brown stain on the seat was dry. When I first got to New York, I would always stand on the subway. But I'd quickly realised that a dirty seat was preferable to being flung around the carriage and bouncing off other commuters when the train jolted left and right.

I got out at Grand Central and walked towards the UN building, marvelling at this enormous, wide structure covered in concrete and glass. On a sunny day, it served as a huge mirror to the city, with silhouettes of the skyscrapers reflecting off its windows, and the East River shimmering just behind. I wasn't in a hurry that morning, but I still walked fast, trying to outpace others around me all heading to the same place. I could tell they worked at the UN by the dark-blue lanyards around their necks. Hanging from them was a rectangular, lighter-blue-coloured ID card in a thick plastic cover, which we used to get inside and move around the UN building. It was like an elite village, where everyone could tell your level of importance by the letter on your blue pass. If you were a diplomat, your ID would have a big 'D' on the front; if you were UN staff, it would have 'S'. As an NGO representative, mine said 'N', although I often joked with colleagues that it stood for 'No', the answer we mostly got when trying to enter any of the meeting rooms.

As I crossed the road just in front of the UN building, I looked up and found myself face to face with a tall man who had a large forehead and reading glasses halfway down his nose. I recognised him immediately as the Syrian ambassador to the UN. Bashar Jaafari was a long-time Syrian politician and diplomat. He was fiercely loyal to President al-Assad; when the war first broke out and other ambassadors were defecting and joining the opposition, Jaafari never wavered. Our eyes met for a moment and I froze, staring at him with my mouth open as he hurried past to the other side of the road.

I was angry at myself for not saying something smart, waving my finger at him, snarling at him, anything! But the brief encounter also made me think about the kind of access I had by being at the UN and representing Amnesty. Al-Assad had placed his most skilled and loyal diplomat here to protect himself against any backlash and to allow him to keep committing war crimes. That meant he feared what the UN could do. It meant there was power here. I just needed to find a creative solution to the problem of the Russian veto.

'You need to speak to Jörn,' was the answer I got from Renzo Pomi, my colleague at Amnesty who had been working in the UN office for 20 years and often gave me advice when I was stuck. Renzo had spent a lot of time teaching me the rules of the UN and sharing his contacts with me. He was a gentle soul with a quick wit that always took me by surprise.

'Who's Jörn?' I asked apologetically.

'A diplomat at the mission of Liechtenstein,' Renzo replied, turning his chair away from his computer to look at me.

'Liechtenstein?! Is that really a country?' I shot back, instantly regretting the question.

'Well, it was invented by Disney, but the UN decided to make it a member state,' Renzo said drily. I looked blank, and he continued: 'I'm joking. Liechtenstein is an Alpine microstate next to Switzerland. You could actually drive through the whole country and not notice it; there are only maybe 50,000 people living there. But it does have its own princes and princesses.'

At the UN, where size really does matter, I came to learn that Liechtenstein is a complete anomaly. Its ambassador, Christian

Wenaweser, has held his position at the UN since 2002 and knows everyone in and everything about the place. The information in his head is not the kind you can find in a book; it's acquired over decades of dealing with ambassadors, secretary-generals, special envoys, and so on. Despite the formalities and rules at the UN, a lot of what happens there is a consequence of precedents that were set in other situations. Knowing how certain events played out in the past, and having that information at your fingertips, is gold. That is Ambassador Wenaweser's superpower, along with his two young and highly intelligent advisors, Sina Alavi and Jörn Eiermann. Together, they are the underrated, overachieving A-team of the UN.

I reached out to Jörn, and we agreed to meet the following day at a French restaurant and bakery often frequented by UN staffers and diplomats because of its proximity to the UN building. I walked in, scanning the room for either a bald or a white head. Given his reputation, I had imagined an older, spectacle-wearing man, perhaps with a leather satchel.

'Sherine? I recognised you from your picture. I just googled you. I'm Jörn,' said an excited male voice with a distinct German accent.

He can't be, he's younger than I am, I thought silently. Jörn had big blue eyes and soft blond hair that flopped over the front of his face, covering one eye. He was slim and tall and was wearing skinny blue jeans and a crisp white dress shirt with a thin tie. He smiled widely and invited me to take a seat.

I launched straight into Syria, where the situation had deteriorated further, with President al-Assad's forces taking over a rebel stronghold in the city of Aleppo, and running battles between rebel fighters and government forces backed up by Russian missiles. The UN, and specifically High Commissioner al-Hussein's office, had evidence that forces loyal to the government were gunning down ordinary people and killing them in their homes. Amnesty was documenting similar incidents.

'In fact, we have a new report we are about to release that proves ...' I trailed off when I noticed Jörn was wincing and looking around him.

'This place is full of, um, colleagues,' he said. 'Let's walk and talk.'

We bought sandwiches from the bakery counter and headed out. I wasn't sure if I was meant to continue telling him about our upcoming report on Aleppo. Jörn took the lead and started making small talk about New York and how much he was enjoying living in such a bustling city after growing up in a small German town.

As soon as we were out of earshot, Jörn apologised for stopping me abruptly. He explained that diplomats and security personnel from other countries had listened in on his conversations in that restaurant before.

'We are working with the Qataris on an idea for Syria. It's big,' he said excitedly, pausing to enjoy the look on my face. I was nodding vigorously at him to continue, eager for more details.

'The Canadian resolution had a lot of good stuff in it, but it wasn't enough.'

Jörn was referring to a Canadian resolution that had been adopted by the General Assembly a week earlier, calling for an end to the targeting of civilians. It was a triumph at the time even to get the General Assembly to meet on Syria, but as a non-binding resolution it was doing nothing to end the attacks or help the people of Aleppo.

'We want to get the General Assembly to pass a resolution setting up an entirely new mechanism, designed specifically to collect evidence of the crimes being committed in Syria and investigate them. We are calling it the International, Impartial and Independent Mechanism for Syria.'

He had my attention. Calling on the Syrian regime and other parties to stop the violence was one thing, setting something up to ensure they were held responsible was another: it could actually prevent them from committing further crimes. Our own researchers at Amnesty had long been telling me how worried they were because they had no access to the areas where the atrocities were taking place. Most of the evidence would likely be gone by the time they reached them, making it near impossible to ever hold anyone accountable.

'I didn't realise the General Assembly had the authority to create something like that,' I said carefully.

'Well, that's a matter of interpretation, according to Ambassador Wenaweser. But we are not worried about that. The General Assembly has a lot of power. This mechanism isn't a court; its job will be to collect, preserve, and prepare the evidence for prosecution by other courts.'

He was making sense, so much so that I was sceptical — if this was true, then why had nobody else thought about it earlier? The Syrian war was in its sixth year.

'I guess you think you have the votes, but how do you guarantee the states who voted for the Canadian resolution at the General Assembly will do the same for yours, and create a whole new mechanism?'

Jörn nodded and took a big bite of his sandwich. 'There are

no guarantees, but that's where Amnesty comes in,' he replied, chewing thoughtfully.

He explained that the benefit of the Canadian resolution was that it got countries, particularly African and Caribbean ones, to vote in favour of a resolution on a specific country. In the past, that had been a tall ask, because countries feared that once the General Assembly started calling out individual states, theirs could be next. But the situation was deteriorating so fast in Syria that many states felt a responsibility to intervene.

'We want to put this resolution up for a vote in two weeks, before the Christmas break. Which means we will need help with outreach to ensure the votes,' Jörn said.

We needed a majority of the 193 countries to come on board for the resolution to pass, which was no easy task. Liechtenstein may be well respected at the UN, but it is still a microstate and therefore doesn't have much leverage over other countries. But Jörn had a plan, and his determination left no room for hesitation. He explained that we would need to divide the member states of the General Assembly into their regional groupings, and then take out the ones we knew would never vote in favour — Russia, China, Syria, North Korea, and their allies. That still left dozens of governments we would have to convince.

Jörn and I kept in close touch for the next few days, sharing information from diplomats, and how the votes were tallying up. One of the big regional groups I was helping to lobby was the Latin American and Caribbean bloc. In 2016, the group was led by Brazil, whose representatives were not very keen on our idea to set up a new mechanism. Their concern was financial; the new mechanism would need tens of thousands of dollars to get started, and that burden would be shared among those who supported it. Perhaps, they suggested, we should wait a few more months.

The Brazilians weren't the only ones trying to slow us down. The UK, which had been supportive of action on Syria at the Security Council, was trying to set up its own accountability mechanism focusing solely on crimes committed by the Islamic State in Syria and Iraq. It was pressuring us to wait until after its own mechanism was set up. But Jörn and Ambassador Wenaweser were adamant it was now or never. Waiting was dangerous, because it would give those opposed to the mechanism time to find ways to pressure countries into voting against it.

Together with Jörn and some others from supportive states, we called ambassadors and met with diplomats at coffee shops and wherever else they chose. The key was to try to actually speak to and connect with each person we were lobbying. It sounds obvious, but when you have a long list of diplomats to contact, it's tempting to send out mass emails. A copy-and-paste approach was not going to work. We needed to address specific concerns with each diplomat and secure votes verbally.

I was hesitant at first, worried that my lack of lobbying experience and legal knowledge would catch me out. But I quickly realised that I had something more useful than legal arguments: during my reporting days, I had witnessed first-hand the suffering of Syrian refugees and heard them recount the horrors they had witnessed; I had felt the ground shake beneath my feet as I watched airstrikes destroy entire neighbourhoods and leave people with nothing. In the sterile environment of the UN, I tried to bring in some reality of how bad the situation really was. I also realised that I was just good at communicating; specifically, I was good at articulating an argument quickly, confidently, and convincingly. That was the essence of lobbying, and television news had given me a lot of practice.

One frustrating morning, a week before the vote was called, I complained to Jörn that a diplomat whose country was still on the fence about how to vote was insisting he had no time for me.

'Tell him you will walk him to his next meeting,' he advised, 'and don't take no for an answer.'

I did as Jörn said, and finally the diplomat agreed to let me escort him from his office across the road to the UN building. I had less than a minute to convince him. While desperately trying not to get run over, I argued that the mechanism was not only the way finally to get justice for Syrians, but would also act as a deterrent for the regime and other parties to stop committing human rights violations. The diplomat's response was one I was hearing a lot, even among those who had voted in favour of the Canadian resolution earlier in the month: 'The mechanism violates state sovereignty.'

State sovereignty is another one of those ubiquitous terms used widely at the UN. The argument made by governments is that although the aim is to work together at the UN, and set up basic global rules or standards that all governments abide by, countries maintain their right to make decisions for their citizens as they see fit.

This struggle between acting in your country's best interest and the collective good of all people is a tricky balance, and it sits at the very heart of the debate over the need for multilateral bodies like the UN. I gave the diplomat my well-rehearsed counter-argument. 'This isn't about taking away Syria's — or any other country's — sovereignty. The second paragraph of the resolution reaffirms that principle, and the primary burden to investigate and prosecute these crimes rests with the Syrian government,' I assured him.

As he hurried through the doors, leaving me behind the security barrier, I was at least pleased with myself for having been well prepared. In readiness to counter his arguments, I had spent the previous evening reading and listening to past statements that he and his colleagues had made about the conflict in Syria. I wasn't sure I had got through to him, but he had promised to relay my arguments.

In the meantime, Amnesty mobilised an army of advocates in our offices around the world to speak to diplomats in their own countries and convince them to support the resolution. It was vital that we all had the same message and were prepared for any question the politicians might have. If an official would not commit to voting for the resolution, the advocate would feed that information back to me in New York so that I could try on my end. Where necessary, we spoke to local journalists about our concerns, to try to get the public to apply pressure to their governments. As the images coming out of Aleppo grew worse and worse daily, the sustained pressure of our lobbying began to create a groundswell of momentum.

Days before Christmas, the General Assembly adopted Resolution 248, establishing the International, Impartial and Independent Mechanism for Syria (IIIM). One hundred and five states voted in favour of the resolution, including the country whose diplomat I had lobbied crossing the street. It was a resounding victory.

Jörn and I met the next afternoon in the park near our office, and I thanked him for all he had done. I had learned so much from him in the last few weeks, not just about how to construct a convincing argument, but also how hard work and preparation pay off. The creation of the mechanism was a small win on a long road to justice, but I was learning that advocacy was all about the consistency and energy we put into every step along the way. I wondered if the IIIM would have been created if Jörn had not believed in it so strongly.

We sat in silence for a few minutes, taking in the moment and how we had been a small part of an historic day for the General Assembly and for Syria.

'So, it turns out the UN isn't useless,' I said eventually.

He sat back on the bench, straightening his legs in front of him and smiling up at the sky.

'Not today,' he replied.

15.

The Trump Distraction

I sat on my sofa, mindlessly swiping through photos of men on my phone, as my mother leaned over me to see the screen.

'This one looks nice,' she said. I looked up at her, my eyebrows raised. She was more excited about this dating app than I was.

'I'd never have guessed when I was a young girl that one day we would be sitting in New York and you would be helping me find a date,' I replied.

She laughed and took the phone from me to continue scrolling, frustrated that her long, manicured nails were getting in the way of finding my true love.

Since my break-up and decision to leave journalism, I had become a lot closer to my mother. She'd visited me several times in New York, and we went out for dinners together and hung out at home like best friends. Perhaps our relationship had improved because now she wasn't constantly worrying about my safety, and

we were finally able to talk about things besides my next deployment. She had also confided in me that she felt guilty about her
part in what had happened with my former fiancé. There was a
lot I hadn't told her about my relationship at the time, a lot of
moments in which I had chosen silence over honesty. She made
me promise after I moved to New York not to keep any secrets
from her, and I happily agreed.

'What does it mean, "No Trumpers"?' she asked, turning to
face me. I explained the guy meant that he didn't want to date
women who were supporters of the newly elected President Trump.

'Ah, strange thing to write on your profile,' she remarked.

Donald Trump had just been inaugurated and it felt like it
was all the entire country was talking about. In New York, where
Trump supporters were in the minority, the initial sadness at his
election had quickly turned to anger. Suddenly, everyone had
strong views on politics, and they were spilling over into every
interaction. I needed a break. I swiped away the No Trumpers guy.

The truth was, as entertaining as it was for my mother and
friends, online dating was exhausting. I had only been on a few
actual dates, but they had all been different versions of disaster.
The first guy I met for a coffee accidentally dropped a condom
packet on the floor between us as he reached his hand out of his
pocket to greet me. Not a good start. Another one talked inces-
santly for almost an hour before asking me to remind him of my
name. Almost nobody let me speak for more than a few minutes.
After weeks of dating, I hadn't wanted to see any of them a second
time. I'd come close once, before the guy texted me saying: 'Just
checking you're not still hoping to have a kid. I know you're 37 so
that dream must be over?!' I never saw him again.

It felt good to be able to talk, and laugh, with my mother and Leila about my dating adventures. But there was also a sadness that accompanied the end of each one. Even when I thought I had no expectations, the realisation, usually within the first few minutes of the date, that he was not *the one* left me feeling down and even more lonely. Each date felt like I was failing at love, rather than getting closer to finding it.

I decided to distract myself with work, and with Trump in office there was plenty of it. The UN had been awash with rumours even before he'd taken office about US plans to cut funding. The US is the biggest contributor in the world to the UN's budget — under President Obama the previous year, the US had contributed around 1.3 billion dollars. Trump was now proposing a fraction of that amount. He made clear that he simply didn't understand what the UN was doing for Americans. But there was another reason why Trump disliked the UN, and it was pretty simple — he didn't want to have to play by any rules that he hadn't made.

Towards the end of Trump's first year in office, he decided to recognise Jerusalem as the capital of Israel, in what became known as his Jerusalem declaration. This was controversial because it was common understanding that the status of Jerusalem would be determined in a final peace settlement between Israel and the Palestinians. To add fuel to the flames, Trump also announced plans to move the US embassy in Israel from Tel Aviv to Jerusalem.

The news reverberated around the world, inciting protests in the Middle East, and became the main topic of discussion at the UN. Trump's declaration was not just reversing nearly seven decades of US policy, it was sticking a middle finger up at the international community and over 30 years of fragile diplomacy between Israel and the Palestinians. It felt like every diplomat inside the UN building was talking about Trump's utter disregard for international law. Despite the fact that he had promised during his election campaign to move the embassy if elected, it seemed no one had thought he would actually go through with it.

The declaration made our interactions with Trump officials at the UN even more awkward and hostile. Trump's ambassador to the UN at the time, Nimrata 'Nikki' Haley, was a staunch ally of Israel and applauded the Jerusalem decision. A former governor of South Carolina, Haley had little experience in international affairs and desperately tried to shut down any discussion about the Jerusalem declaration at the UN.

I had met Haley months before the declaration, at a private meeting with a few other NGOs, following her trip to visit Syrian refugees in Lebanon. She had walked into the room that day, surrounded by her aides, wearing an expensive-looking electric-blue suit. She greeted me by sandwiching my hand between hers and leaning in when we spoke, as if she was intent on what I was saying. The overall effect, paired with her deep southern accent, was surprisingly charismatic and warm. She had already earned a reputation for being incredibly ambitious and savvy, despite big knowledge gaps on world politics. She told us about her impressions of the refugee camps in great detail, and gave us rehearsed lines about how important our work was on the ground. But by the time it came to her questions, it was clear she wasn't aware of the difference between those of us representing humanitarian groups, focused on running aid programmes on the ground, and those of us from human rights organisations, whose main work is documenting violations of international law and seeking justice. Haley was unapologetic about what she didn't know, and didn't seem to notice or care about the confused looks she was getting, even from her own staff. She had the kind of confidence I had seen in world leaders.

Haley took as her own the fight with the UN over Trump's recognition of Jerusalem. At the Security Council in December 2017, she vetoed a draft resolution calling for a withdrawal of Donald Trump's decision in a 14–1 vote, leaving the US completely isolated and Haley out of sync with her fellow ambassadors from other countries. Two days later, the president of the General Assembly called an emergency session to vote on a resolution criticising President Trump's decision.

It was my first opportunity since Trump had made his Jerusalem announcement to actually do some advocacy. My team and I called and met with UN diplomats, explaining the importance of the vote and the dangers of Trump's move. It wasn't a difficult task; most of those we spoke to were planning on voting for the resolution. Despite the normal hesitancy of many smaller states to vote against the US, there was a feeling among diplomats that the US president had gone too far, and that somehow this vote was against Trump's rejection of international norms, rather than against the US per se.

Nikki Haley got on the podium before the vote and warned states that the US was 'taking names' of those who planned to vote for the resolution. She and her team had mounted a massive lobbying effort to try to convince states to vote with the US. Haley's 'I'm warning you' schoolteacher threat at the General Assembly was typical of her approach. A week before,

I had been called on my mobile by a senior aide of Haley's expressing his displeasure at my tweets about the ambassador and her lack of knowledge of international law when it came to the Israeli–Palestinian conflict. I offered to brief the ambassador on the subject, but the man on the phone was only interested in scolding me, saying that my name had been noted down at the mission, and menacingly hinting he would block my access to the UN building. At one point, he indicated that he had looked into me and that perhaps I was taking the whole Jerusalem thing too personally because of my Middle Eastern heritage.

These bullying tactics didn't work on anyone. The resolution passed overwhelmingly and sent a message that the US's decision was not shared by the rest of the world. Trump's move had inadvertently triggered a show of support for the Palestinians greater than any seen in years, if ever. In an effort to save face, Haley held a reception for her allies, beefing up the numbers by counting among the supporters those states that had abstained or failed to turn up for the vote.

But despite gains at the UN, the situation for many Palestinians continued to deteriorate as a result of plans to move the embassy. In Gaza, tens of thousands protested along the border fence with Israel, and in a single day 58 Palestinians were killed after Israeli forces opened fire on them. Israel claimed it was responding to rocket fire. It was the bloodiest single day in Gaza for years, and once the death toll hit 120, the Security Council decided to meet and vote on a resolution calling for international protections for civilians in Gaza.

My colleagues and I waited for hours inside the Security Council on the afternoon of the Gaza vote. I was sitting alone on the folding seats in the NGO-assigned area at the back of the chamber. I was getting used to being relegated to the furthest and most uncomfortable seats in the room. I was also being careful to avoid eye contact with the guard, realising he was the same one who had thrown me out of the chamber a week earlier for sneakily eating a bagel.

I watched the diplomats run around the horseshoe table, whispering in each other's ears, holding briefs in their hands and looking very serious. This went on for several minutes, and it was clear that something was afoot. At one point, Nikki Haley was kneeling on the floor next to an ambassador, looking like she was pleading with him. Minutes later, I saw her mouthing the word 'please' to the Peruvian ambassador, looking solemn with her hand on her chest. Haley knew she would use her veto to kill the resolution, but she didn't want to be the only person casting a 'no' vote. When the Israeli ambassador came into the chamber, Haley embraced him warmly, kissing him on both cheeks, before he too was taken into a huddle. I was watching live lobbying in action — right now, Haley's job was not so different from my own. Just then, one by one, the diplomats started to disappear behind a door at the back of the chamber. The Russian ambassador, who was the president of the Security Council at the time, had called for what's known as 'closed consultations', a private meeting in which the resolutions would be negotiated away from the cameras.

A diplomat friend who was in the chamber later told me that Haley and her team were trying to convince the other members to accept all the changes she had made to the Gaza resolution. But the Russian ambassador said the changes were absurd. The diplomat told me that Haley's team had struck out so many sentences and written so many notes on the draft that you could barely see a word of the original. The Russian ambassador told Haley that the only solution was for her to present her own resolution.

If Haley had been more experienced, she would have rejected the idea outright. Although UN ambassadors are the ones who negotiate and cast the vote on behalf of their country, ultimately the decision on which way to vote on important resolutions like this one had to be made back in capitals by ministers or even heads of state. By suddenly forcing a vote on a completely new resolution that nobody had time to run past their bosses back home, it would be dead in the water.

As predicted, the US used its veto to block the original resolution. Then came the vote on Haley's resolution, which received just one vote — Haley's. It was another diplomatic humiliation, even for the Trump administration, who prided themselves on not caring what the international community thought of them. Once again, on the heels of the General Assembly resolution, the US looked alone and outplayed. The Palestinian ambassador later told the press that Haley's attempt was an 'epic failure' unlike anything he had seen in the history of the UN Security Council.

Throughout the day, I was tweeting what was going on in the chamber. I was struck by how Haley had adopted the Israeli military lingo for describing the situation, painting a picture of Israel having no option but to defend itself from a territory full of terrorists. The dehumanisation of Palestinians in Gaza was nothing new — I had seen it over and over again in my reporting career — but faced with it at the UN, I could see what a powerful legal defence it provided for Israel's supporters.

After the vote, I got a message from an old colleague in Gaza. He had been following my tweets and said that the whole thing was making him lose hope. He sent me a photo of the view outside his apartment of a demolished building. Below were kids playing football, using a cardboard box as a goal. 'Meanwhile, this is what Gaza looks like,' he wrote.

Despite the theatrics, the days of negotiating and lobbying had achieved nothing for Palestinians still living under siege and occupation. Again, more people were dying, and the reaction was little more than words of sympathy from a few of the ambassadors during the meeting. It may have been a diplomatic win for the Palestinian leadership that day at the UN, but how many people in Gaza would even know about it? Even those who had access to a TV had more pressing concerns than the actions of a few bureaucrats thousands of miles away.

It was clear that the ability of the US, as well as Russia and China, to veto resolutions with seemingly no cost was rendering the Security Council useless. I looked up at the giant mural on the back wall of the chamber. Renzo had told me it was an oil painting by a Norwegian artist that had been there since the early 1950s. At the centre of the painting was a rising phoenix, surrounded by dark, hell-like images of war and suffering in deep red and black. Above the phoenix were lighter-coloured images of smiling families. It was meant to show the UN's role in bringing a brighter future. But that day, all it symbolised to me was how out of touch the Council was and how far it had strayed from the reason it was created: to maintain peace and bring security.

The Jerusalem debacle also brought to the surface

conversations about our role as NGOs at the UN, trying to affect policy from the back seats. One of the most challenging aspects of the job was how to get the Security Council to respond to crisis and urgent human rights situations quickly enough. The result was that the body was always out of step in its reactions. By the time the member states got around to discussing a situation, it had already reached a dangerous stage. The Council would only decide to meet when the situation clearly needed a strong and unified statement; it would only release a statement when it should have been adopting a resolution. The body was not just out of sync when it came to situations in the Middle East like Syria or Palestine; the problem was much wider, particularly when one of the veto-wielding powers had a stake in a conflict.

This issue came up again in the late summer of 2017, when we started hearing reports from Myanmar about soldiers going into villages belonging to the minority Muslim community called the Rohingya, and burning them to the ground. A friend of mine, an experienced human rights investigator called Tirana Hassan, who at the time was head of the crisis team at Amnesty, immediately flew to neighbouring Bangladesh, where refugees from Myanmar were crossing the border on foot, carrying all their belongings. Amnesty had been monitoring the situation closely for the last few weeks, ever since a Rohingya armed group had killed Myanmar soldiers in an ambush. But reports coming out of Bangladesh that tens of thousands of people were fleeing made us aware that the crisis had entered a new phase.

One Friday evening, just I was leaving work, Tirana called me from Bangladesh.

'I don't have much time to talk, but things are worse here than

I have ever seen. We have to do something about this. Right now.'

Tirana was born a straight talker. It was easy to work with her because she could be both politically pragmatic and passionately principled about human rights. Tirana explained that the num-bers crossing the border were enormous and growing, and that the stories she was hearing, especially from women, were horrific.

'I spoke to a woman with four children. She told me that when the soldiers started burning her village, she had to choose which of her children to save and which to leave behind, because she couldn't carry all of them on her back.'

I stopped, and the person behind crashed into me, cursing as he passed. I couldn't move as I listened to Tirana tell me more stories she was hearing, of babies being thrown into fires by angry soldiers, women being raped, and whole villages being razed to the ground.

'I've covered so many awful stories in my time, Sherine, but this is something else.'

I hung up the phone and called my colleague Lou Charbonneau at Human Rights Watch. I relayed what Tirana had said, and he confirmed he was hearing the same stories from his researchers on the ground.

We worked together through the weekend, making calls and trying to find out what the UN was doing about the situation. China is a big supporter of the Myanmar government and was protecting it from any criticism or action. Days were passing, and the Security Council couldn't even agree to meet and discuss the situation.

Amnesty and Human Rights Watch decided to call a joint press conference at the UN to ask the Security Council to meet urgently in public, demand the military stop the killings, and insist they grant access to UN staff to document what was happening. If there was one thing my advocacy work had shown me, whether in Egypt or at the UN, it was the importance of working in coalition with other groups to amplify the message.

I insisted we patch in Tirana during the press conference to tell us what she was hearing in Bangladesh. This was unusual for UN press conferences, but it was important to make sure what she was documenting was being heard in real time. I thought about the war in Gaza I had covered with Ayman Mohyeldin, and how reminiscent Tirana's stories were and the feeling that nobody was listening. I could hear the horror and desperation in her voice: it was just like mine almost ten years ago. Now, I was in a position to call for something to be done. It was an enormous responsibility, but it was exactly why I had joined Amnesty. This time, it was my job to do something about the horrors someone else was witnessing.

Dozens of media outlets and diplomats turned up to our press conference, which was broadcast around the world. Lou and I explained the background to the violence our researchers were documenting, including the anti-Rohingya propaganda that had incited the population in Myanmar, and the decades of repression and system of apartheid that had led to this moment.

Tirana called the situation unprecedented, with 340,000 refugees crossing the border. She called out the indiscriminate and widespread nature of the killings of civilians, and referred to what the military was doing, including the mass burning of villages, as collective punishment. She knew that it was important to describe what she was seeing as deliberate and premeditated

— part of a plan to empty the area of the Rohingya population, which had to be stopped. Another colleague from HRW said the situation had the hallmarks of ethnic cleansing. We showed the journalists satellite images we had collected of over 20 areas that had been affected by widespread burnings. Tirana said that she could see the smoke from the border billowing for days due to the extent of the burnings.

The following day, the Security Council met in private to discuss the situation. Some members broke their silence after being questioned aggressively by the same journalists who had been at our press conference. The diplomats said they were concerned about the excessive violence being used by security forces. It took another two weeks for the Council to meet in public, after the UN secretary-general intervened. By that time, the major news networks were all over the story of the atrocities being committed in Myanmar, including sexual attacks by Myanmar soldiers against Rohingya women and girls.

As I was finishing up work one evening, I got another call from Tirana. She was back home in France after a week of travel to meet with politicians and policymakers in different countries, where she described the evidence she and her team had gathered and tried to convince them to stop supporting Myanmar, and the generals responsible for overseeing the atrocities in particular. They were the same names she had come across years earlier when working in Myanmar during previous rounds of violence against the Rohingya. We talked about what to do next, and which new calls we could make to the international community. I ran her through a list of ideas I had come up with to try to regain the momentum. Despite the initial buzz from the press conference and the reaction of some UN diplomats, attention was starting to wane, while the situation for the Rohingya was as grim as ever, with little hope of the hundreds of thousands who had fled their homes being able to return anytime soon. There was some talk of possibly setting up another mechanism, like the one we had created for Syria, and of ambassadors visiting Myanmar and Bangladesh to see for themselves what was going on.

I sat back on my chair, alone in the Amnesty office, strategising with Tirana while looking out of the window at UN headquarters. The snipers were positioning themselves on the roof of the Security Council, ready to protect the gathering world leaders. It was the eve of my second opening of the UN General Assembly, and I was again questioning what more we should be doing — this time to find a way around the Chinese veto.

'It will never feel like you're doing enough. If it does, then you're doing the job wrong,' Tirana said, before telling me she was exhausted and hanging up. I realised it was the middle of the night in France.

I thought about my colleagues, like Tirana, who dedicated their lives to helping others and making the world a little fairer and more just. For some of them, being an activist was a choice. For others, their circumstances — perhaps having to advocate for a loved one — had created the activist in them. But what they all had in common was a formidable, unrelenting energy, which they used to change the seemingly immovable.

I opened up my laptop again and printed out the page of ideas

I had just been discussing with Tirana. I wasn't sure if any of them were good enough or could make a real difference. A voice in my head was telling me that most of them weren't even feasible, given China's influence and veto power. I persisted, though, making my way down the list, writing in the margins who would be a good ally for each idea and coming up with a timeline to build up to key moments. The more I researched and wrote, the lower the voice in my head became, and I remembered the words of my friend Alaa Abd el-Fattah: 'As for the activists, we always find a way.'

I kept scribbling down my thoughts until the lights went out in our building, signalling it was about to close up for the night. By the time I was done, I had handwritten another five pages, including a detailed plan to stick images of the generals in Myanmar on the pavement around the UN in time for the start of UNGA Leaders' Week. Imagine politicians from all around the world awkwardly jumping over the slabs of concrete to try to avoid stomping on the generals' faces, I thought. If we could find a way to keep reminding everyone of what was happening in Myanmar, make the story follow the generals around everywhere they went, like a black stain, just like we had done to President el-Sisi when my colleagues had been jailed, maybe in time we could change their actions. We could force them to recalculate the risk of continuing with their plan to rid the country of the Rohingya people. We could save lives.

As I packed up my things, I still wondered if there was more I could be doing, but I realised that I had stopped asking myself whether I was in the right place. Nowadays, my job didn't make me feel like I had after Gaza, walking away from the conflict overwhelmed by guilt and sadness, and it didn't fill me with defeat and deflation like working in Cairo had. In journalism, my success had depended on delivering a product as fast as possible and moving on. Advocacy was different; progress could be very slow and difficult to measure. But even if my mission would always feel incomplete, that was better than the unfulfilling finality I had felt for so many years as a journalist.

In the process of making change, we all have different roles to play. As I made my way home that night, I knew it wasn't perfect, but that I had found mine.

16.

So, What's Next?

The chanting was so loud, it was as if the protestors were standing around my bed.

I shot up, grabbed my phone from the charger, and rushed to the big window facing the street, muttering to myself along the way. Lunchtime naps were pretty much the only thing about the pandemic-induced work-from-home regimen that I enjoyed, and I wasn't happy about being woken up.

A few dozen or so demonstrators were below, shouting angrily. In front of them was a line of police officers in full riot gear, brandishing shields.

My apartment in Brooklyn shares a wall with the local police station. When I was buying it, I thought that would be an advantage. Added security for a single woman in a big city, I told my mother when she came with me to see it. She agreed, probably relieved to hear me finally taking my own safety seriously. Now, the decision didn't seem so smart. I could see more protestors hurriedly turning the corners and heading to the police station from both sides of the street, racing against the officers dragging metal fence cordons to block them off.

My phone rang; it was Ayman.

'Are you home? We can hear the protestors from here. Come over when you can.'

Ayman and Kenza had moved from their apartment overlooking the river and bought a much bigger house just down the road from mine. I waited until I could see a clear path out, grabbed my face mask, and took the longer way round through the backstreets. On my way, I passed through even more crowds of protestors marching and chanting in unison.

'Black Lives Matter,' one man shouted through a megaphone, almost singing it.

'Black Lives Matter,' repeated the crowds, echoing his tone, but with even more volume and determination. They were mainly young men and women holding signs saying '#BLM', 'I can't breathe', and 'Justice for George'. George Floyd was a 46-year-old Black man who was killed by police officer Derek Chauvin. Chauvin knelt on Floyd's neck for over nine minutes while Floyd, handcuffed and face down on the floor, repeated, 'I can't breathe.' Floyd had been arrested on suspicion of using a counterfeit $20 bill. The murder was caught on video, which quickly went viral, prompting protests in the US and around the world against police brutality and institutional racism.

I hurried over to Ayman and Kenza's house and let myself in, finding them sitting at the table, chatting, with giant mugs of hot tea. I relaxed as I took in the familiar deep, woody scent of the oud oils that they liked to burn. Their new home reminded me of a modern, less cluttered version of Number 29. It was tall and narrow and filled with art, books, and furniture collected from all over the Middle East. They had bought the house just before their second child was born. When the pandemic hit soon after, and once the initial lockdown restrictions eased, it became an oasis for all of us.

I greeted the kids, who were playing on the other side of the room, made myself herbal tea and assumed my regular seat next to Ayman at the table.

'It's kind of strange, this slogan: "Black Lives Matter", I said, trying to articulate something I'd been thinking about. In my years of reporting on protests, I had got used to seeing slogans that began 'Down with so and so' or 'End something'. These were statements of anger, clear and directional. But simply saying that Black lives mattered ... Only a statement that stark and seemingly undisputable could convey the true complexity — and persistence — of racial injustice.

The first book I read when I moved to New York was Ta-Nehisi Coates's *Between the World and Me*. Written as a letter from Coates to his teenage son, warning him of the perils of being a Black boy growing up in this country, I stayed up all night reading his vivid descriptions of the racist attitudes that still exist in America. I somehow had the impression before I came to the US that the country had reckoned with its racist past. I quickly realised how wrong I was, and that racism was very much present in everyday life, as well as in institutions like the police force.

Black Lives Matter (BLM) is an organisation founded by three Black women in 2013 following the acquittal of the man who shot dead 17-year-old Trayvon Martin. Ayman had followed its evolution and was explaining its significance.

'It's completely changed the conversation around race in this country. Not just as an organisation but also as a grassroots movement,' he said, as he joined his wife in trying to block off the section of the sofa that had become their son's new launch pad. 'We've never had these kinds of discussions before, or devoted this much airtime to issues of race and discrimination,' he continued.

They both looked exhausted. Despite the COVID-19 restrictions, Ayman was still going into the MSNBC studios every day to anchor the news. Between the pandemic and the protests, it had turned into one of the most relentless news cycles in years.

As I made my way home that evening, I thought about the eruption in activism. This moment resonated for so many people on various levels. Debate about endemic racism within the police force had led to conversations among many ordinary people about how to confront our own unconscious bias. Friends and family who had scarcely shown any interest in social justice were now messaging me, expressing their outrage and sharing articles about how to be more conscious of discrimination and privilege. There seemed to be a painful reckoning going on, as many people woke up to their own bias and acknowledged their part in perpetuating inequality.

It made me think about my own biases, the ideas I held as a result of my class and privilege. Ideas that had a bearing on almost every decision I made, from whom I befriended to where I chose to live. It also made me reflect on the prejudice I had experienced myself, and how often I had brushed it aside. As a child in London, I'd grown up among protests like these against discriminatory policies and police brutality. But my parents had worked hard to shield me from overt racism, to pretend nothing was happening when our neighbour shouted racist slurs at my father. Back then, my mother had explained it away as her being 'unwell'. Perhaps that was how my parents really saw it: racism as an illness without logic or solution. Or perhaps, like so many other immigrant families, they felt ashamed to admit that they were victims of bigotry.

But the BLM moment also highlighted another type of racism, which was just as unacceptable. The subtle, everyday microaggressions that people of colour are subjected to in many societies. Every time we are singled out for being different, whether it's negative attention — like me losing out on a job because of my non-existent foreign accent — or when it is supposedly positive, such as being praised for having 'exotic' looks or 'interesting' hair. The result is often to make us feel different, isolated, and disempowered.

Seeing these overt and covert biases, and witnessing the extreme social injustice in Egypt growing up, had been two of the most important factors that had driven me to want to confront discrimination in all its forms, in journalism and, later, through human rights work. It made injustice un-ignorable. It made it personal.

One morning, I woke up to a message from one of my young cousins in London. He had been posting on his social media about the BLM protests and now he asked me directly, 'So, what can I do?' I called him, and as we spoke it became clear that he was serious about doing more than just sharing photos of protests online. I told him to imagine a world where racism didn't exist and start working to create it. The key to activism, I explained, was to stay active — reading and learning more about an issue, coming up with ideas, calling, writing, emailing, collecting, and sharing information, using everyone you knew to try to reach decision-makers, and advocating for change even when it felt out of reach. It's hard work, and it's never easy. A few days after we spoke, he sent me a message saying he had started a fundraiser for Floyd's family and was looking into creating a hotline at his college where people could safely report instances of racism.

My cousin wasn't the only one looking for ways to get more involved in the injustices he was seeing. In the US, the Trump administration's opposition to everything from Muslims to abortions, paired with the current groundswell of activism, made my job with Amnesty feel more important than ever. Since I had joined the organisation, I had been focused on working with the UN to address the fallout from major armed conflicts around the world. But now there was another type of war brewing right on my doorstep: a battle for acknowledgement of and action on entrenched inequality. As a campaigning organisation focused on bringing justice, Amnesty had a role in this moment to work with the newly activated crowds of people, not just in the US but around the world.

The challenge for us was to figure out how to harness some of this new energy and channel it into making real change, rather than letting it dissipate after people had gone to a protest or 'liked' a few posts and moved on. It was on a Zoom call with my team during the protests that I realised just how difficult this was going to be. One by one, my colleagues were briefing the senior director on what they were planning. Ideas were put forward to organise protests around various themes or write opinion pieces for major publications. But the response from our boss to almost every idea was: 'Isn't that already being done?' The truth was that it was hard for Amnesty to find its place in this moment. Traditionally, we would have been organising protests and stunts, sending out instructions about where to meet or which banner to bring, but now anyone with a phone seemed to be doing that. 'So, what are we doing that's adding value?' the director kept asking, while the rest of us looked down and kept our mute button on.

Events were forcing us all to think quickly about our role in making a change. Within a few days of the Zoom call, we had a plan. The Trump administration and his supporters were claiming that cracking down on the BLM protests was fair and legal, but we were going to challenge that. We dispatched researchers all over the country to document the tactics and actions of the police against the protestors. By the summer of 2020, we had collected and analysed hundreds of videos and photos, and documented over 100 separate examples of police violence against protestors in 40 states. It was the most comprehensive report published on the subject at the time.

Using this information, we were able to show objectively why police reform was so necessary, and how widespread the problem of unjustified violence against protestors was across the country. We battled the campaign of mass disinformation being spread by the Trump administration with actual facts, and used that information to inform our calls for policy change. We also connected people from all over the world so that they could share their experiences of police brutality, and tactics for confronting it in their countries. Our message to them was simple: You are not alone and, yes, you can make a difference. By the next Zoom call with our director, there were no awkward silences, rather a burst of ideas on how to follow up on the report and make sure we were activating our ten million supporters around the world to call for police reform. Not everything we tried succeeded — many of our calls, like demilitarising the police, were ignored. But we stayed active, pushing for policy change state by state, locally and incrementally. The combined action and advocacy coming from so many people, politicians, influencers, and organisations led to the revision of police guidelines in some states and the banning of certain problematic police protocols. In a historic verdict, Derek Chauvin was charged with second-degree murder and sentenced to 22 years and six months in prison. Three other officers were charged with violating Floyd's civil rights.

As the protests started to fade and the news cycle moved on, the real legacy of the killings that sparked global BLM protests appears to be the way in which they forced many to think about their own role in perpetuating racism, as well as their obligation to end it. Ignoring the problem is no longer an option. Companies and organisations, including Amnesty, are requiring staff to undergo anti-racism training. Amnesty itself had to confront complaints from staff on a problematic culture of white privilege.

There is no doubt that much, much more still needs to be done in the US and around the world to address the imbalance and bias, not just in law enforcement but also economically, socially, and culturally. But the new way of thinking and questioning unleashed by the BLM movement has left an imprint on a generation, and it is up to all of us to decide what lasting effect that will have.

On the first anniversary of the murder of George Floyd, I was scrolling through my social media and found a post from my young cousin. He had put up a photo of his fundraiser, which had raised thousands of dollars, and below it a list of all the organisations in the UK that were still working on the issue of racism and police brutality, encouraging his friends to get involved. He noticed that I was online and messaged me. 'So, what's next? I want to do more,' he wrote.

I smiled, thinking of the journey he was about to embark on, and perhaps also feeling a little less alone in mine.

'Welcome to activism,' I wrote back.

Postscript

We all ask children what they want to *be* when they grow up. We almost never ask them what they want to *do*. Too often, we don't ask them to think about what contribution they want to make to the world, or empower them to believe they can change it.

Changing the world seems too large a task. Society tries to shame us into thinking we're naïve for even attempting to make a difference. That is for others to do, those with power and influence. Not us normal people.

I grew up with this mentality, watching reporters on television, thinking I could never be in their place; seeing starving kids in Cairo slums and feeling that something was wrong but that it wasn't in my power to change it.

But over the years, my work has taught me that even if your role appears tiny and inconsequential in comparison to the magnitude of the situation you are trying to affect, everyone can play a part in changing the world. It just takes enough of us to care.

My life did not go as planned; I am not married with three children, nor am I a doctor or a lawyer or part of the other 'approved' professions so often prescribed to aspirational women from immigrant families like mine. But by accepting who I am and recognising the part of me that longed to dedicate myself to activism, I changed my life and found fulfilment. I even eventually fell in love again, this time with someone who makes me feel consistently valued, understood, and safe, and whose two wonderful children have transformed my life. I am surrounded by love, have a deep and honest relationship with my parents, and a job I passionately believe in, even if I often still think I should be doing more.

I don't have the perfect life or career, but I have found happiness by being honest about what I want. Making choices in the absolute belief that although I am only one person, I can make a difference. That I need not be a bystander. That I can be someone who strives to change the world — one small act at a time.

Acknowledgements

First, to the incredible women in my life:

Rawya Rageh, Leila Fadel, Sonia Dridi, Rula Amin, Tirana Hassan, Hannah Allam, Abigail Hauslohner, Vivian Salama, Hadeel al-Shalchi, Heba Morayef, Lulu Garcia-Navarro, Lina Attalah, Jacky Rowland, Nisreen el-Shamayleh, Nadia Abouel Magd, Dareen Abu Ghaida, Rosie Garthwaite, Tamara Bralo, Amal Hamdan, Carrie Seim, Kenza Fourati, Mari Griffin, Yoonie Kim, Rebecca Teitel, Alia Malek, Taghreed al-Khodary, Dena Takruri, Arwa Damon, Amber Fares, Marcia Biggs, Jenifer Vaughan, Yasmin el-Rifae, Emma Bowen, Lila Nejad, Maureen Suter, Mayssa Daye, and Dina Selim.

Thank you for proving that it was never about being fearless, but about being determined.

To my family: Ihab, Sylvia, Rania, Rafeek, Daniel, Marian, Matthew, Yasmine, Lara, and Adam. This book is as much your story as mine. I hope I did us justice.

To my friend Ayman Mohyeldin, who has gone on to achieve the kind of success we dreamed about as rookie reporters. I remain your biggest fan.

To my agent, Elias Altman, for believing in the importance of my story and fiercely defending my right to tell it; and to the wonderful team at Scribe UK, especially Sarah and Simon, for navigating the thoughts in my head on to the page with skill and patience.

And finally, to my loves: Eric, Jackson, and Riley. You helped me find home again.